THE BOOK OF
WEREWOLVES

THE WERE WOLVES.

THE BOOK OF
WEREWOLVES

SABINE BARING-GOULD

Introduction by
NIGEL SUCKLING

SENATE

The Book of Werewolves

First published in 1865 by Smith, Elder & Co., London

This edition published in 1995 by Senate, an imprint of
Studio Editions Ltd, Princess House, 50 Eastcastle Street,
London W1N 7AP, England

ISBN 1 85958 072 6
Printed and bound in Guernsey by
The Guernsey Press Co Ltd

INTRODUCTION

First published in 1865, Sabine Baring-Gould's classic study of werewolves is a revelation on the subject, being written at a time when werewolves were still taken very seriously in the wilder corners of Europe and, indeed, most other parts of the world. Since then, werewolves have retreated into fiction and famously into films where, along with vampires, they have become purveyors of macabre entertainment. But what this book demonstrates is that the werewolf was once the object of very real terror. And with good reason.

The spark of this study was Baring-Gould's close encounter in the remote French countryside with, if not quite the creature itself, a first-hand and very solid belief in its existence. (He describes this belief in an opening worthy of a Gothic novel.) This led him to wonder about the roots of the belief and thus to an investigation which trawls an enormous range of sources dating from antiquity up to the nineteenth century, skipping lightly from Norse saga to African and American folktales.

The author's own position is robustly modern, couched though it is in the leisurely and polished language of his day. The viewpoint to which he regularly returns is that lycanthropy, the condition of being a werewolf, is primarily a mental disorder often accompanied by hallucinations in both sufferers and their victims. But in his various digressions he builds a strong case for something much more tangible than this, giving a chilling taste of the reality of the condition for those in its thrall and for whom scepticism and urbane detachment were as remote as the moon.

Lycanthropy was a criminal offence in much of Europe during the late Middle Ages and those convicted of it usually met a horrible end. The records of such cases, almost because of their legal soberness, provide much of Baring-Gould's most disturbing and fascinating material. In the light this the story of *Little Red Riding Hood* changes from a cautionary poetic fable into a worryingly direct warning of what was liable to happen to children who went straying in the woods.

Bloodthirstiness, cruelty, shapeshifting and cannibalism all come under examination, both as manifested in werewolves and in a wider context. Given his subject, the author's curiosity is almost by definition slightly morbid, but he stops short of salaciousness. The true stories he tells are terrible enough without the finer grisly details, in particular that of Gilles de Laval, also known as the

Maréchal de Letz, whose tale was here presented to the English reading public for the first time with any accuracy.

And grim reading it makes too. The Maréchal was also known as 'Bluebeard', under which soubriquet he passed rapidly into folklore. But the *true* story as related in some detail by Baring-Gould is hardly less fantastic and is told with a verve any storyteller of old would admire. Champion of France against the English in the fifteenth century, marshall, councillor and chamberlain to the king, lord of wide estates in Brittany and possessor of a vast fortune, the Maréchal nevertheless ended his life on a fiery gallows amid one of the scandals of the century. His dark appetites had been woken, he claimed, by his reading of the cruelties practiced by the ancient Caesars whom he sought to emulate.

One by one the author carefully examines the various strands of the werewolf legend and many of his conclusions are as valid today as when he was writing. For example, one theory has it that lycanthropy is simply one form of a human condition quite able to adopt other guises. Reading the examples in this book, many modern parallels spring to mind.

As wild wolves died out on the margins of

civilization, so too did the fear of werewolves. But under different masks they continue to prowl in our midst, stunning the world from time to time when they are exposed.

Sabine Baring-Gould (1834-1924) brought an immense authority and energy to his subject as well as an interesting viewpoint, for he was by profession a parson as well as a celebrated author, archaeologist and folklorist. One of the foremost collectors of British folksongs, he also composed the famous anthem *Onward Christian Soldiers*, published a monumental sixteen-volume edition of *Lives of the Saints* in addition to about thirty novels and a hundred other books on a wide range of topics. This combination of talents endows his study of werewolves with an enduring quality which has rarely been matched.

For developments of the legend since the nineteenth century one has to look elsewhere, but for its foundation this, the first in-depth examination in the English language, remains almost necessary reading. One only wishes it were longer.

Nigel Suckling
1994

CONTENTS

Chapter IV

The Origin of the Scandinavian Were-wolf

Chapter V

The Were-wolf in the Middle Ages

Chapter VI

A Chapter of Horrors

Chapter VII

Jean Grenier

Chapter VIII

Folk-Lore Relating to Were-wolves

Chapter IX

Natural Causes of Lycanthropy

Chapter X

Mythological Origin of the Were-wolf Myth

CONTENTS

CHAPTER XI

THE MARÉCHAL DE REZT I: THE INVESTIGATION OF CHARGES

CHAPTER XII

THE MARÉCHAL DE REZT II: THE TRIAL

CHAPTER XIII

MARÉCHAL DE RETZ III: THE SENTENCE AND EXECUTION

CHAPTER XIV

A GALICIAN WERE-WOLF

Chapter XV

ANOMALOUS CASE – THE HUMAN HYÆNA

CHAPTER XVI

A SERMON ON WERE-WOLVES

THE

BOOK OF WERE-WOLVES

THE

BOOK OF WERE-WOLVES.

CHAPTER I.

INTRODUCTORY.

I SHALL never forget the walk I took one night in
Vienne, after having accomplished the examination of an
unknown Druidical relic, the Pierre labie, at La Ron-
delle, near Champigni. I had learned of the existence of
this cromlech only on my arrival at Champigni in tho
afternoon, and I had started to visit the curiosity
without calculating the time it would take me to reach
it and to return. Suffice it to say that I discovered the
venerable pile of grey stones as the sun set, and that I
expended the last lights of evening in planning and
sketching. I then turned my face homeward. My

1

walk of about ten miles had wearied me, coming at the
end of a long day's posting, and I had lamed myself
in scrambling over some stones to the Gaulish relic.

A small hamlet was at no great distance, and I
betook myself thither, in the hopes of hiring a trap to
convey me to the posthouse, but I was disappointed.
Few in the place could speak French, and the priest,
when I applied to him, assured me that he believed
there was no better conveyance in the place than a
common charrue with its solid wooden wheels; nor
was a riding horse to be procured. The good man
offered to house me for the night; but I was obliged
to decline, as my family intended starting early on the
following morning.

Out spake then the mayor—"Monsieur can never
go back to-night across the flats, because of the—the—"
and his voice dropped; "the loups-garoux."

"He says that he must return!" replied the priest
in patois. "But who will go with him?"

"Ah, ha! M. le Curé. It is all very well for one
of us to accompany him, but think of the coming back
alone!"

"Then two must go with him," said the priest,
"and you can take care of each other as you return."

"Picou tells me that he saw the were-wolf only this day se'nnight," said a peasant; "he was down by the hedge of his buckwheat field, and the sun had set, and he was thinking of coming home, when he heard a rustle on the far side of the hedge. He looked over, and there stood the wolf as big as a calf against the horizon, its tongue out, and its eyes glaring like marsh-fires. Mon Dieu! catch me going over the marais to-night. Why, what could two men do if they were attacked by that wolf-fiend?"

"It is tempting Providence," said one of the elders of the village; "no man must expect the help of God if he throws himself wilfully in the way of danger. Is it not so, M. le Curé? I heard you say as much from the pulpit on the first Sunday in Lent, preaching from the Gospel."

"That is true," observed several, shaking their heads.

"His tongue hanging out, and his eyes glaring like marsh-fires!" said the confidant of Picou.

"Mon Dieu! if I met the monster, I should run," quoth another.

"I quite believe you, Cortrez; I can answer for it that you would," said the mayor.

"As big as a calf," threw in Picou's friend.

"If the loup-garou were *only* a natural wolf, why then, you see"—the mayor cleared his throat—"you see we should think nothing of it; *but,* M. le Curé, it is a fiend, a worse than fiend, a man-fiend,—a worse than man-fiend, a man-wolf-fiend."

"But what is the young monsieur to do?" asked the priest, looking from one to another.

"Never mind," said I, who had been quietly listening to their patois, which I understood. "Never mind; I will walk back by myself, and if I meet the loup-garou I will crop his ears and tail, and send them to M. le Maire with my compliments."

A sigh of relief from the assembly, as they found themselves clear of the difficulty.

"Il est Anglais," said the mayor, shaking his head, as though he meant that an Englishman might face the devil with impunity.

A melancholy flat was the marais, looking desolate enough by day, but now, in the gloaming, tenfold as desolate. The sky was perfectly clear, and of a soft, blue-grey tinge; illumined by the new moon, a curve of light approaching its western bed. To the horizon reached a fen, blacked with pools of stagnant water, from which the frogs kept up an incessant trill through the summer night. Heath and fern covered the ground, but near the water grew dense masses of flag and bul_rush, amongst which the light wind sighed wearily. Here and there stood a sandy knoll, capped with firs, looking like black splashes against the grey sky; not a sign of habitation anywhere; the only trace of men being the white, straight road extending for miles across the fen.

That this district harboured wolves is not improbable, and I confess that I armed myself with a strong stick at the first clump of trees through which the road dived.

This was my first introduction to were-wolves, and the circumstance of finding the superstition still so prevalent, first gave me the idea of investigating the history and the habits of these mythical creatures.

I must acknowledge that I have been quite unsuccessful in obtaining a specimen of the animal, but I have found its traces in all directions. And just as the palæontologist has constructed the labyrinthodon out of its foot-prints in marl, and one splinter of bone, so may this monograph be complete and accurate, although I have no chained were-wolf before me which I may sketch and describe from the life.

The traces left are indeed numerous enough, and though perhaps like the dodo or the dinormis, the werewolf may have become extinct in our age, yet he has left his stamp on classic antiquity, he has trodden deep in Northern snows, has ridden rough-shod over the mediævals, and has howled amongst Oriental sepulchres. He belonged to a bad breed, and we are quite content to be freed from him and his kindred, the vampire and the ghoul. Yet who knows! We may be a little too hasty in concluding that he is extinct. He may still prowl in Abyssinian forests, range still over Asiatic steppes, and be found howling dismally in some padded room of a Hanwell or a Bedlam.

In the following pages I design to investigate the notices of were-wolves to be found in the ancient writers of classic antiquity, those contained in the Northern Sagas, and, lastly, the numerous details afforded by the mediæval authors. In connection with this I shall give a sketch of modern folklore relating to Lycanthropy.

It will then be seen that under the veil of mythology lies a solid reality, that a floating superstition holds in solution a positive truth.

This I shall show to be an innate craving for blood implanted in certain natures, restrained under ordinary circumstances, but breaking forth occasionally, accompanied with hallucination, leading in most cases to cannibalism. I shall then give instances of persons thus afflicted, who were believed by others, and who believed themselves, to be transformed into beasts, and who, in the paroxysms of their madness, committed numerous murders, and devoured their victims.

I shall next give instances of persons suffering from the same passion for blood, who murdered for the mere gratification of their natural cruelty, but who were not subject to hallucinations, nor were addicted to cannibalism.

I shall also give instances of persons filled with the same propensities who murdered and ate their victims, but who were perfectly free from hallucination.

CHAPTER II.

LYCANTHROPY AMONG THE ANCIENTS.

Definition of Lycanthropy—Marcellus Sidetes—Virgil—Herodotus—
Ovid—Pliny—Agriopas—Story from Petronius—Arcadian Legends
—Explanation offered.

WHAT is Lycanthropy? The change of man or woman
into the form of a wolf, either through magical means,
so as to enable him or her to gratify the taste for human
flesh, or through judgment of the gods in punishment
for some great offence.

This is the popular definition. Truly it consists in
a form of madness, such as may be found in most
asylums.

Among the ancients this kind of insanity went by
the names of Lycanthropy, Kuanthropy, or Boanthropy,
because those afflicted with it believed themselves to be
turned into wolves, dogs, or cows. But in the North of
Europe, as we shall see, the shape of a bear, and in

Africa that of a hyæna, were often selected in prefer-
ence.   A mere matter of taste ! According to Marcellus
Sidetes, of whose poem περὶ λυκανθρώπου a fragment
exists, men are attacked with this madness chiefly in
the beginning of the year, and become most furious
in February; retiring for the night to lone cemeteries, and living precisely in the manner of dogs and
wolves.

Virgil writes in his eighth Eclogue :—

> Has herbas, atque hæc Ponto mihi lecta venena
> Ipse dedit Mœris; nascuntur plurima Ponto.
> His ego sæpe lupum fieri, et se conducere sylvis
> Mœrim, sæpe animas imis excire sepulchris,
> Atque satas alio vidi traducere messes.

And Herodotus :—" It seems that the Neuri are sorcerers, if one is to believe the Scythians and the
Greeks established in Scythia; for each Neurian changes
himself, once in the year, into the form of a wolf,
and he continues in that form for several days, after
which he resumes his former shape."—(Lib. iv.
c. 105.)

See also Pomponius Mela (lib. ii. c. 1): " There is a
fixed time for each Neurian, at which they change, if
they like, into wolves, and back again into their former
condition."

But the most remarkable story among the ancients is that related by Ovid in his "Metamorphoses," of Lycaon, king of Arcadia, who, entertaining Jupiter one day, set before him a hash of human flesh, to prove his omniscience, whereupon the god transferred him into a wolf:—*

> In vain he attempted to speak; from that very instant
> His jaws were bespluttered with foam, and only he thirsted
> For blood, as he raged amongst flocks and panted for slaughter.
> His vesture was changed into hair, his limbs became crooked;
> A wolf,—he retains yet large trace of his ancient expression,
> Hoary he is as afore, his countenance rabid,
> His eyes glitter savagely still, the picture of fury.

Pliny relates from Evanthes, that on the festival of Jupiter Lycæus, one of the family of Antæus was selected by lot, and conducted to the brink of the Arcadian lake. He then hung his clothes on a tree and plunged into the water, whereupon he was transformed into a wolf. Nine years after, if he had not tasted human flesh, he was at liberty to swim back and resume his former shape, which had in the meantime become aged, as though he had worn it for nine years.

Agriopas relates, that Demænetus, having assisted

---

* OVID. *Met.* i. 237; PAUSANIAS, viii. 2, § 1; TZETZE *ad Lycoph.* 481; ERATOSTH. *Catas.* i. 8.

at an Arcadian human sacrifice to Jupiter Lycæus, ate of the flesh, and was at once transformed into a wolf, in which shape he prowled about for ten years, after which he recovered his human form, and took part in the Olympic games.

The following story is from Petronius :—

" My master had gone to Capua to sell some old clothes. I seized the opportunity, and persuaded our guest to bear me company about five miles out of town ; for he was a soldier, and as bold as death. We set out about cockcrow, and the moon shone bright as day, when, coming among some monuments, my man began to converse with the stars, whilst I jogged along singing and counting them. Presently I looked back after him, and saw him strip and lay his clothes by the side of the road. My heart was in my mouth in an instant, I stood like a corpse ; when, in a crack, he was turned into a wolf. Don't think I'm joking : I would not tell you a lie for the finest fortune in the world.

" But to continue : after he was turned into a wolf, he set up a howl and made straight for the woods. At first I did not know whether I was on my head or my heels ; but at last going to take up his clothes, I found them turned into stone. The sweat streamed

from me, and I never expected to get over it. Melissa
began to wonder why I walked so late. 'Had you come
a little sooner,' she said, 'you might at least have lent
us a hand; for a wolf broke into the farm and has
butchered all our cattle; but though he got off, it was
no laughing matter for him, for a servant of ours ran
him through with a pike. Hearing this I could not
close an eye; but as soon as it was daylight, I ran
home like a pedlar that has been eased of his pack.
Coming to the place where the clothes had been turned
into stone, I saw nothing but a pool of blood; and
when I got home, I found my soldier lying in bed, like
an ox in a stall, and a surgeon dressing his neck. I
saw at once that he was a fellow who could change his
skin (*versipellis*), and never after could I eat bread
with him, no, not if you would have killed me. Those
who would have taken a different view of the case are
welcome to their opinion; if I tell you a lie, may your
genii confound me!"

As every one knows, Jupiter changed himself into a
bull; Hecuba became a bitch; Actæon a stag; the
comrades of Ulysses were transformed into swine; and
the daughters of Prœtus fled through the fields believing themselves to be cows, and would not allow any

one to come near them, lest they should be caught and yoked.

S. Augustine declared, in his *De Civitate Dei*, that he knew an old woman who was said to turn men into asses by her enchantments.

Apuleius has left us his charming romance of the *Golden Ass*, in which the hero, through injudicious use of a magical salve, is transformed into that long-eared animal.

It is to be observed that the chief seat of Lycanthropy was Arcadia, and it has been very plausibly suggested that the cause might be traced to the following circumstance :—The natives were a pastoral people, and would consequently suffer very severely from the attacks and depredations of wolves. They would naturally institute a sacrifice to obtain deliverance from this pest, and security for their flocks. This sacrifice consisted in the offering of a child, and it was instituted by Lycaon. From the circumstance of the sacrifice being human, and from the peculiarity of the name of its originator, rose the myth.

But, on the other hand, the story is far too widely spread for us to attribute it to an accidental origin, or to trace it to a local source.

Half the world believes, or believed in, were-wolves, and they were supposed to haunt the Norwegian forests by those who had never remotely been connected with Arcadia: and the superstition had probably struck deep its roots into the Scandinavian and Teutonic minds, ages before Lycaon existed; and we have only to glance at Oriental literature, to see it as firmly engrafted in the imagination of the Easterns.

CHAPTER III.

THE WERE-WOLF IN THE NORTH.

Norse Traditions—Manner in which the Change was effected—Vœlundar Kvœda—Instances from the Völsunga Saga—Hrolfs Saga Kraka—Faroëse Poem—Helga Kvida—Vatnsdæla Saga—Eyrbyggja Saga.

IN Norway and Iceland certain men were said to be *eigi einhamir,* not of one skin, an idea which had its roots in paganism. The full form of this strange superstition was, that men could take upon them other bodies, and the natures of those beings whose bodies they assumed. The second adopted shape was called by the same name as the original shape, *hamr,* and the expression made use of to designate the transition from one body to another, was *at skipta hömum,* or *at hamaz ;* whilst the expedition made in the second form, was the *hamför.* By this transfiguration extraordinary powers were acquired; the natural strength of the individual was doubled, or quadrupled; he acquired the strength of the beast in whose body he travelled, in addition to his own, and a man thus invigorated was called *hamrammr*.

The manner in which the change was effected, varied. At times, a dress of skin was cast over the body, and at once the transformation was complete; at others, the human body was deserted, and the soul entered the second form, leaving the first body in a cataleptic state, to all appearance dead. The second hamr was either borrowed or created for the purpose. There was yet a third manner of producing this effect—it was by incantation; but then the form of the individual remained unaltered, though the eyes of all beholders were charmed so that they could only perceive him under the selected form.

Having assumed some bestial shape, the man who is *eigi einhammr* is only to be recognized by his eyes, which by no power can be changed. He then pursues his course, follows the instincts of the beast whose body he has taken, yet without quenching his own intelligence. He is able to do what the body of the animal can do, and do what he, as man, can do as well. He may fly or swim, if he is in the shape of bird or fish; if he has taken the form of a wolf, or if he goes on a *gandreið*, or wolf's-ride, he is full of the rage and malignity of the creatures whose powers and passions he has assumed.

I will give a few instances of each of the three methods of changing bodies mentioned above. Freyja and Frigg had their falcon dresses in which they visited different regions of the earth, and Loki is said to have borrowed these, and to have then appeared so precisely like a falcon, that he would have escaped detection, but for the malicious twinkle of his eyes. In the Vælundar kviða is the following passage : —

I.	I.
Meyjar flugu sunnan	From the south flew the maidens
Myrkvið igögnum	Athwart the gloom,
Alvitr unga	Alvit the young,
Orlög drýgja;	To fix destinies;
þær á sævarströnd	They on the sea-strand
Settusk at hvilask,	Sat them to rest,
Dró sir suðrœnar	These damsels of the south
Dýrt lín spunnu.	Fair linen spun.

II.	II.
Ein nam þeirra	One of them took
Egil at verja	Egil to press,
Fögr mær fíra	Fair maid, in her
Faðmi ljósum;	Dazzling arms.
Önnur var Svanhvít,	Another was Svanhwit,
Svanfjaðrar dró;	Who wore swan feathers;
En in þriðja	And the third,
þeirra systir	Their sister,
Var i hvítan	Pressed the white
Háls Völundar.	Neck of Vœlund.

The introduction of Sœmund tells us that these charming young ladies were caught when they had laid their swan-skins beside them on the shore, and were consequently not in a condition to fly.

In like manner were wolves' dresses used. The following curious passage is from the wild Saga of the Völsungs :—

" It is now to be told that Sigmund thought Sinfjötli too young to help him in his revenge, and he wished first to test his powers; so during the summer they plunged deep into the wood and slew men for their goods, and Sigmund saw that he was quite of the Völsung stock. . . . Now it fell out that as they went through the forest, collecting monies, that they lighted on a house in which were two men sleeping, with great gold rings on them; they had dealings with witchcraft, for wolf-skins hung up in the house above them; it was the tenth day on which they might come out of their second state. They were kings' sons. Sigmund and Sinfjötli got into the habits, and could not get out of them again, and the nature of the original beasts came over them, and they howled as wolves—they learned both of them to howl. Now they went into the forest, and each took his own course; they made the agreement together that they should try their strength against as many as seven men, but not more, and that he who was ware of strife should utter his wolf's howl.

" ' Do not fail in this,' said Sigmund, ' for you are young and daring, and men would be glad to chase you.' Now each went his own course; and after that they had parted Sigmund found men, so he howled; and when Sinfjötli heard that, he ran up and slew them all—then they separated. And Sinfjötli had not been long in the wood before he met with eleven men; he fell upon them and slew them every one. Then he was tired, so he flung himself under an oak to rest. Up came Sigmund and said, ' Why did you not call out?' Sinfjötli replied, ' What was the need of asking your help to kill eleven men?'

" Sigmund flew at him and rent him so that he fell, for he had bitten through his throat. That day they could not leave their wolf-forms. Sigmund laid him on his back and bare him home to the hall, and sat beside him, and said, ' Deuce take the wolf-forms!' "—Völsunga Saga, c. 8.

There is another curious story of a were-wolf in the same Saga, which I must relate.

"Now he did as she requested, and hewed down a great piece of timber, and cast it across the feet of those ten brothers seated in a row, in the forest; and there they sat all that day and on till night. And at midnight there came an old she-wolf out of the forest to them, as they sat in the stocks, and she was both huge and grimly. Now she fell upon one of them, and bit him to death, and after she had eaten him all up, she went away. And next morning Signy sent a trusty man to her brothers, to know how it had fared with them. When he returned he told her of the death of one, and that grieved her much, for she feared it might fare thus with them all, and she would be unable to assist them.

"In short, nine nights following came the same she-wolf at midnight, and devoured them one after another till all were dead, except Sigmund, and he was left alone. So when the tenth night came, Signy sent her trusty man to Sigmund, her brother, with honey in his hand, and said that he was to smear it over the face of Sigmund, and to fill his mouth with it. Now he went to Sigmund, and did as he was bid, after which he returned home. And during the night came the same she-wolf, as was her wont, and reckoned to devour him, like his brothers.

"Now she snuffed at him, where the honey was smeared, and began to lick his face with her tongue, and presently thrust her tongue into his mouth. He bore it ill, and bit into the tongue of the she-wolf; she sprang up and tried to break loose, setting her feet against the stock, so as to snap it asunder: but he held firm, and ripped the tongue out by the roots, so that it was the death of the wolf. It is the opinion of some men that this beast was the mother of King Siggeir, and that she had taken this form upon her through devilry and witchcraft."—(c. 5.)

There is another story bearing on the subject in the Hrolfs Saga Kraka, which is pretty; it is as follows:—

"In the north of Norway, in upland-dales, reigned a king called Hring; and he had a son named Björn. Now it fell out that the queen died, much lamented by the king, and by all. The people advised him to marry again, and so he sent men south to get him a wife. A gale and fierce storm fell upon them, so that they had to turn the helm, and run before the wind, and so they came north to Finnmark, where they spent the winter. One day they went inland, and came to a house in which sat two beautiful women, who greeted them well, and inquired whence they had come. They replied by giving an account of their journey and their errand, and then asked the women who they were, and why they were alone, and far from the haunts of men, although they were so comely and engaging. The elder replied —that her name was Ingibjorg, and that her daughter was called Hvit, and that she was the Finn king's sweetheart. The messengers decided that they would return home, if Hvit would come with them and marry King Hring. She agreed, and they took her with them and met the king who was pleased with her, and had his wedding feast made, and said that he cared not though she was not rich. But the king was very old, and that the queen soon found out.

"There was a Carle who had a farm not far from the king's dwelling; he had a wife, and a daughter, who was but a child, and her name was Bera; she was very young and lovely. Björn the king's son, and Bera the Carle's daughter, were wont, as children, to play together, and they loved each other well. The Carle was well to do, he had been out harrying in his young days, and he was a doughty champion. Björn and Bera loved each other more and more, and they were often together.

" Time passed, and nothing worth relating occurred; but Björn, the king's son, waxed strong and tall; and he was well skilled in all manly exercises.

"King Hring was often absent for long, harrying foreign shores, and Hvit remained at home and governed the land. She was not liked of the people. She was always very pleasant with Björn, but he cared little for her. It fell out once that the King Hring went abroad, and he spake with his queen that Björn should remain at home with her, to assist in the government, for he thought it advisable, the queen being haughty and inflated with pride.

" The king told his son Björn that he was to remain at home, and rule the land with the queen; Björn replied that he disliked the plan, and that he had no love for the queen; but the king was inflexible, and left the land with a great following. Björn walked home after his conversation with the king, and went up to his place, ill-pleased and red as blood. The queen came to speak with him, and to cheer him; and spake friendly with him, but he bade her be off. She obeyed him that time. She often came to talk with him, and said how much pleasanter it was for them to be together, than to have an old fellow like Hring in the house.

" Björn resented this speech, and struck her a box
in the ear, and bade her depart, and he spurned her
from him.   She replied that this was ill-done to drive
and thrust her away : and ' You think it better, Björn,
to sweetheart a Carle's daughter, than to have my love
and favour, a fine piece of condescension and a disgrace
it is to you !   But, before long, something will stand in
the way of your fancy, and your folly.'   Then she struck
at him with a wolf-skin glove, and said, that he should
become a rabid and grim wild bear; and ' You shall eat
nothing but your father's sheep, which you shall
slay for your food, and never shall you leave this
state.'

" After that, Björn disappeared, and none knew what
had become of him ; and men sought but found him
not, as was to be expected.   We must now relate how
that the king's sheep were slaughtered, half a score at a
time, and it was all the work of a grey bear, both huge
and grimly.

" One evening it chanced that the Carle's daughter
saw this savage bear coming towards her, looking tenderly at her, and she fancied that she recognized the
eyes of Björn, the king's son, so she made a slight
attempt to escape ; then the beast retreated, but she

followed it, till she came to a cave. Now when she entered the cave there stood before her a man, who greeted Bera, the Carle's daughter; and she recognized him, for he was Björn, Hring's son. Overjoyed were they to meet. So they were together in the cave awhile, for she would not part from him when she had the chance of being with him; but he said that this was not proper that she should be there by him, for by day he was a beast, and by night a man.

"Hring returned from his harrying, and he was told the news, of what had taken place during his absence; how that Björn, his son, had vanished, and also, how that a monstrous beast was up the country, and was destroying his flocks. The queen urged the king to have the beast slain, but he delayed awhile.

"One night, as Bera and Björn were together, he said to her :—'Methinks to-morrow will be the day of my death, for they will come out to hunt me down. But for myself I care not, for it is little pleasure to live with this charm upon me, and my only comfort is that we are together; but now our union must be broken. I will give you the ring which is under my left hand. You will see the troop of hunters to-morrow coming to seek me; and when I am dead go to the king, and ask him to give you what is under the beast's left front leg. He will consent.'

"He spoke to her of many other things, till the bear's form stole over him, and he went forth a bear. She followed him, and saw that a great body of hunters had come over the mountain ridges, and had a number of dogs with them. The bear rushed away from the cavern, but the dogs and the king's men came upon him, and there was a desperate struggle. He wearied many men before he was brought to bay, and had slain all the dogs. But now they made a ring about him, and he ranged around it, but could see no means of escape, so he turned to where the king stood, and he seized a man who stood next him, and rent him asunder; then was the bear so exhausted that he cast himself down flat, and, at once, the men rushed in upon him and slew him. The Carle's daughter saw this, and she went up to the king, and said,—' Sire! wilt thou grant me that which is under the bear's left fore-shoulder?' The king consented. By this time his men had nearly flayed the bear; Bera went up and plucked away the ring, and kept it, but none saw what she took, nor had they looked for anything. The king asked her who she was, and she gave a name, but not her true name.

"The king now went home, and Bera was in his company. The queen was very joyous, and treated her well, and asked who she was; but Bera answered as before.

"The queen now made a great feast, and had the bear's flesh cooked for the banquet. The Carle's daughter was in the bower of the queen, and could not escape, for the queen had a suspicion who she was. Then she came to Bera with a dish, quite unexpectedly, and on it was bear's flesh, and she bade Bera eat it. She would not do so. 'Here is a marvel!' said the queen; 'you reject the offer which a queen herself deigns to make to you. Take it at once, or something worse will befall you.' She bit before her, and she ate of that bite; the queen cut another piece, and looked into her mouth; she saw that one little grain of the bite had gone down, but Bera spat out all the rest from her mouth, and said she would take no more, though she were tortured or killed.

"'Maybe you have had sufficient,' said the queen, and she laughed."—(Hrolfs Saga Kraka, c. 24-27, condensed.)

In the Faroëse song of Finnur hin friði, we have the following verse :—

Hegar íð Finnur hetta sær,	When this peril Finn saw,
Mannspell var at meini,	That witchcraft did him harm,
Skapti hann seg í varglíki:	Then he changed himself into a were-wolf :
Hann feldi allvæl fleiri.	He slew many thus.

The following is from the second Kviða of Helga Hundingsbana (stroph. 31) :—

> May the blade bite,
> Which thou brandishest
> Only on thyself, when it
> Chimes on thy head.
> Then avenged will be
> The death of Helgi,
> When thou, as a wolf,
> Wanderest in the woods,
> Knowing nor fortune
> Nor any pleasure,
> Having no meat,
> Save rivings of corpses.

In all these cases the change is of the form : we shall now come to instances in which the person who is changed has a double shape, and the soul animates one after the other.

The Ynglinga Saga (c. 7) says of Odin, that "he changed form; the bodies lay as though sleeping or dead, but he was a bird or a beast, a fish, or a woman, and went in a twinkling to far distant lands, doing his

own or other people's business." In like manner the
Danish king Harold sent a warlock to Iceland in the
form of a whale, whilst his body lay stiff and stark at
home. The already quoted Saga of Hrolf Krake gives
us another example, where Bödvar Bjarki, in the shape
of a huge bear, fights desperately with the enemy,
which has surrounded the hall of his king, whilst his
human body lies drunkenly beside the embers within.

In the Vatnsdæla Saga, there is a curious account
of three Finns, who were shut up in a hut for three
nights, and ordered by Ingimund, a Norwegian chief,
to visit Iceland and inform him of the lie of the country,
where he was to settle. Their bodies became rigid, and
they sent their souls the errand, and, on their awaking
at the end of three days, gave an accurate description of
the Vatnsdal, in which Ingimund was eventually to
establish himself. But the Saga does not relate whether
these Finns projected their souls into the bodies of
birds or beasts.

The third manner of transformation mentioned, was
that in which the individual was not changed himself,
but the eyes of others were bewitched, so that they
could not detect him, but saw him only under a certain
form. Of this there are several examples in the Sagas ;

as, for instance, in the Hromundar Saga Greypsonar,
and in the Fostbræðra Saga. But I will translate the
most curious, which is that of Odd, Katla's son, in the
Eyrbyggja Saga.—(c. 20.)

" Geirrid, housewife in Mafvahlið, sent word into
Bolstad, that she was ware of the fact that Odd, Katla's
son, had hewn off Aud's hand.

"Now when Thorarinn and Arnkell heard that, they
rode from home with twelve men. They spent the
night in Mafvahlið, and rode on next morning to Holt:
and Odd was the only man in the house.

" Katla sat on the high seat spinning yarn, and she
bade Odd sit beside her; also, she bade her women sit
each in her place, and hold their tongues. ' For,' said
she, ' I shall do all the talking.' Now when Arnkell and
his company arrived, they walked straight in, and when
they came into the chamber, Katla greeted Arnkell,
and asked the news. He replied that there was none,
and he inquired after Odd. Katla said that he had
gone to Breidavik. ' We shall ransack the house
though,' quoth Arnkell. ' Be it so,' replied Katla, and
she ordered a girl to carry a light before them, and
unlock the different parts of the house. All they saw
was Katla spinning yarn off her distaff. Now they

search the house, but find no Odd, so they depart. But when they had gone a little way from the garth, Arnkell stood still and said: 'How know we but that Katla has hoodwinked us, and that the distaff in her hand was nothing more than Odd.' 'Not impossible!' said Thorarinn; 'let us turn back.' They did so; and when those at Holt saw that they were returning, Katla said to her maids, 'Sit still in your places, Odd and I shall go out.'

"Now as they approached the door, she went into the porch, and began to comb and clip the hair of her son Odd. Arnkell came to the door and saw where Katla was, and she seemed to be stroking her goat, and disentangling its mane and beard and smoothing its wool. So he and his men went into the house, but found not Odd. Katla's distaff lay against the bench, so they thought that it could not have been Odd, and they went away. However, when they had come near the spot where they had turned before, Arnkell said, 'Think you not that Odd may have been in the goat's form?' 'There is no saying,' replied Thorarinn; 'but if we turn back we will lay hands on Katla.' 'We can try our luck again,' quoth Arnkell; 'and see what comes of it.' So they returned.

"Now when they were seen on their way back, Katla bade Odd follow her; and she led him to the ash-heap, and told him to lie there and not to stir on any account. But when Arnkell and his men came to the farm, they rushed into the chamber, and saw Katla seated in her place, spinning. She greeted them and said that their visits followed with rapidity. Arnkell replied that what she said was true. His comrades took the distaff and cut it in twain.' 'Come now!' said Katla, 'you cannot say, when you get home, that you have done nothing, for you have chopped up my distaff.' Then Arnkell and the rest hunted high and low for Odd, but could not find him; indeed they saw nothing living about the place, beside a boar-pig which lay under the ash-heap, so they went away once more.

"Well, when they got half-way to Mafvahliŏ, came Geirrid to meet them, with her workmen. 'They had not gone the right way to work in seeking Odd,' she said, 'but she would help them.' So they turned back again. Geirrid had a blue cloak on her. Now when the party was seen and reported to Katla, and it was said that they were thirteen in number, and one had on a coloured dress, Katla exclaimed, 'That troll Geirrid is come! I shall not be able to throw a glamour over their eyes any more.' She started up from her place and lifted the cushion off the seat, and there was a hole and a cavity beneath: into this she thrust Odd, clapped the cushion over him, and sat down, saying she felt sick at heart.

"Now when they came into the room, there were small greetings. Geirrid cast off her the cloak and went up to Katla, and took the seal-skin bag which she had in her hand, and drew it over the head of Katla.* Then Geirrid bade them break up the seat. They did so, and found Odd. Him they took and carried to Buland's head, where they hanged him. . . . But Katla they stoned to death under the headland."

---

* A precaution against the "evil eye." Compare *Gisla Saga Surssonnar*, p. 34. *Laxdæla Saga*, cc. 37, 38.

CHAPTER IV.

THE ORIGIN OF THE SCANDINAVIAN WERE-WOLF.

Advantage of the Study of Norse Literature—Bear and Wolf-skin Dresses—The Berserkir—Their Rage—The Story of Thorir—Passages from the Aigla—The Evening Wolf—Skallagrim and his Son — Derivation of the Words Hamr and Vargr — Laws affecting Outlaws—" To become a Boar "—Recapitulation.

ONE of the great advantages of the study of old Norse or Icelandic literature is the insight given by it into the origin of world-wide superstitions. Norse tradition is transparent as glacier ice, and its origin is as unmistakable.

Mediæval mythology, rich and gorgeous, is a compound like Corinthian brass, into which many pure ores have been fused, or it is a full turbid river drawn from numerous feeders, which had their sources in remote climes. It is a blending of primæval Keltic, Teutonic, Scandinavian, Italic, and Arab traditions, each adding a beauty, each yielding a charm, but each accretion rendering the analysis more difficult.

Pacciuchelli says:—" The Anio flows into the Tiber; pure as crystal it meets the tawny stream, and is lost in it, so that there is no more Anio, but the united stream is all Tiber." So is it with each tributary to the tide of mediæval mythology. The moment it has blended its waters with the great and onward rolling flood, it is impossible to detect it with certainty; it has swollen the stream, but has lost its own identity. If we would analyse a particular myth, we must not go at once to the body of mediæval superstition, but strike at one of the tributaries before its absorption. This we shall proceed to do, and in selecting Norse mythology, we come upon abundant material, pointing naturally to the spot whence it has been derived, as glacial moraines indicate the direction which they have taken, and point to the mountains whence they have fallen. It will not be difficult for us to arrive at the origin of the Northern belief in were-wolves, and the data thus obtained will be useful in assisting us to elucidate much that would otherwise prove obscure in mediæval tradition.

Among the old Norse, it was the custom for certain warriors to dress in the skins of the beasts they had

slain, and thus to give themselves an air of ferocity, calculated to strike terror into the hearts of their foes.

Such dresses are mentioned in some Sagas, without
there being any supernatural qualities attached to them.
For instance, in the Njála there is mention of a man
i geitheðni, in goatskin dress.   Much in the same way
do we hear of Harold Harfagr having in his company a
band of berserkir, who were all dressed in wolf-skins,
ulfheðnir, and this expression, wolf-skin coated, is met
with as a man's name.   Thus in the Holmverja Saga,
there is mention of a Björn, "son of *Ulfheðin*, wolf-
skin coat, son of *Ulfhamr*, wolf-shaped, son of *Ulf*, wolf,
son of *Ulfhamr*, wolf-shaped, who could change forms."

But the most conclusive passage is in the Vatnsdæla Saga, and is as follows:—"Those berserkir who
were called *ulfheðnir*, had got wolf-skins over their
mail coats" (c. xvi.)   In like manner the word *berserkr*,
used of a man possessed of superhuman powers, and
subject· to accesses of diabolical fury, was originally
applied to one of those doughty champions who went
about in bear-sarks, or habits made of bear-skin over
their armour.   I am well aware that Björn Halldorson's
derivation of berserkr, bare of sark, or destitute of
clothing, has been hitherto generally received, but Svei-

björn Egilsson, an indisputable authority, rejects this derivation as untenable, and substitutes for it that which I have adopted.

It may be well imagined that a wolf or a bear-skin would make a warm and comfortable great-coat to a man, whose manner of living required him to defy all weathers, and that the dress would not only give him an appearance of grimness and ferocity, likely to produce an unpleasant emotion in the breast of a foe, but also that the thick fur might prove effectual in deadening the blows rained on him in conflict.

The berserkr was an object of aversion and terror to the peaceful inhabitants of the land, his avocation being to challenge quiet country farmers to single combat. As the law of the land stood in Norway, a man who declined to accept a challenge, forfeited all his possessions, even to the wife of his bosom, as a poltroon unworthy of the protection of the law, and every item of his property passed into the hands of his challenger. The berserkr accordingly had the unhappy man at his mercy. If he slew him, the farmer's possessions became his, and if the poor fellow declined to fight, he lost all legal right to his inheritance. A berserkr would invite himself to any feast, and contribute his quota to the hilarity of the entertainment, by snapping the backbone, or cleaving the skull, of some merrymaker who incurred his displeasure, or whom he might single out to murder, for no other reason than a desire to keep his hand in practice.

It may well be imagined that popular superstition went along with the popular dread of these wolf-and-bear-skinned rovers, and that they were believed to be endued with the force, as they certainly were with the ferocity, of the beasts whose skins they wore.

Nor would superstition stop there, but the imagination of the trembling peasants would speedily invest these unscrupulous disturbers of the public peace with the attributes hitherto appropriated to trolls and jötuns.

The incident mentioned in the Völsunga Saga, of the sleeping men being found with their wolf-skins hanging to the wall above their heads, is divested of its improbability, if we regard these skins as worn over their armour, and the marvellous in the whole story is reduced to a minimum, when we suppose that Sigmund and Sinfjötli stole these for the purpose of disguising themselves, whilst they lived a life of violence and robbery.

In a similar manner the story of the northern "Beauty and Beast," in Hrolf's Saga Kraka, is rendered less improbable, on the supposition that Björn

was living as an outlaw among the mountain fastnesses
in a bearskin dress, which would effectually disguise
him—*all but his eyes*—which would gleam out of the
sockets in his hideous visor, unmistakably human. His
very name, Björn, signifies a bear; and these two circumstances may well have invested a kernel of historic
fact with all the romance of fable; and if divested of
these supernatural embellishments, the story would
resolve itself into the very simple fact of there having
been a King Hring of the Updales, who was at variance
with his son, and whose son took to the woods, and
lived a berserkr life, in company with his mistress, till
he was captured and slain by his father.

I think that the circumstance insisted on by the
Saga-writers, of the eyes of the person remaining un-
changed, is very significant, and points to the fact that
the skin was merely drawn over the body as a disguise.

But there was other ground for superstition to
fasten on the berserkir, and invest them with supernatural attributes.

No fact in connection with the history of the Northmen is more firmly established, on reliable evidence,
than that of the berserkr rage being a species of diabolical possession. The berserkir were said to work

themselves up into a state of frenzy, in which a demoniacal power came over them, impelling them to acts from which in their sober senses they would have recoiled. They acquired superhuman force, and were as invulnerable and as insensible to pain as the Jansenist convulsionists of S. Medard. No sword would wound them, no fire would burn them, a club alone could destroy them, by breaking their bones, or crushing in their skulls. Their eyes glared as though a flame burned in the sockets, they ground their teeth, and frothed at the mouth; they gnawed at their shield rims, and are said to have sometimes bitten them through, and as they rushed into conflict they yelped as dogs or howled as wolves.*

According to the unanimous testimony of the old Norse historians, the berserkr rage was extinguished by baptism, and as Christianity advanced, the number of these berserkir decreased.

But it must not be supposed that this madness or

---

* Hic (Syraldus) septem filios habebat, tanto veneficiorum usu callentes, ut sæpe subitis furoris viribus instincti solerent ore torvum infremere, scuta morsibus attrectare, torridas fauce prunas absumere, extructa quævis incendia penetrare, nec posset conceptis dementiæ motus alio remedii genere quam aut vinculorum injuriis aut cædis humanæ piaculo temperari. Tantam illis rabiem sive sævitia ingenii sive furiarum ferocitas inspirabat.—*Saxo Gramm.* VII.

possession came only on those persons who predisposed themselves to be attacked by it; others were afflicted with it, who vainly struggled against its influence, and who deeply lamented their own liability to be seized with these terrible accesses of frenzy. Such was Thorir Ingimund's son, of whom it is said, in the *Vatnsdœla Saga*, that " at times there came over Thorir berserkr fits, and it was considered a sad misfortune to such a man, as they were quite beyond control."

The manner in which he was cured is remarkable; pointing as it does to the craving in the heathen mind for a better and more merciful creed :—

" Thorgrim of Kornsá had a child by his concubine Vereydr, and, by order of his wife, the child was carried out to perish.

" The brothers (Thorsteinn and Thorir) often met, and it was now the turn of Thorsteinn to visit Thorir, and Thorir accompanied him homeward. On their way Thorsteinn asked Thorir which he thought was the first among the brethren; Thorir answered that the reply was easy, for 'you are above us all in discretion and talent; Jökull is the best in all perilous adventures, but I,' he added, ' I am the least worth of us brothers, because the berserkr fits come over me, quite against my will, and I wish that you, my brother, with your shrewdness, would devise some help for me.'

" Thorsteinn said,—' I have heard that our kinsman, Thorgrim, has just suffered his little babe to be carried out, at the instigation of his wife. That is ill done. I think also that it is a grievous matter for you to be different in nature from other men.'

" Thorir asked how he could obtain release from his affliction . . . . Then said Thorsteinn, ' Now will I make a vow to Him who created the sun, for I ween that he is most able to take the ban off you, and I will undertake for His sake, in return, to rescue the babe and to bring it up for him, till He who created man shall take it to Himself—for this I reckon He will do ! ' After this they left their horses and sought the child, and a thrall of Thorir had found it near the Marram river. They saw that a kerchief had been spread over its face, but it had rumpled it up over its nose; the little thing was all but dead, but they took it up and flitted it home to Thorir's house, and he brought the lad up, and called him Thorkell Rumple; as for the berserkr fits, they came on him no more." (c. 37.)

But the most remarkable passages bearing on our subject will be found in the *Aigla*.

" There was a man, Ulf (the wolf) by name, son of
Bjálfi and Hallbera. Ulf was a man so tall and strong
that the like of him was not to be seen in the land
at that time. And when he was young he was out
viking expeditions and harrying . . . He was a great
landed proprietor. It was his wont to rise early, and
to go about the men's work, or to the smithies, and
inspect all his goods and his acres; and sometimes he
talked with those men who wanted his advice; for he
was a good adviser, he was so clear-headed; however,
every day, when it drew towards dusk, he became so
savage that few dared exchange a word with him, for
he was given to dozing in the afternoon.

" People said that he was much given to changing
form (*hamrammr*), so he was called the evening-wolf,
kveldúlfr."— (c. 1.) In this and the following passages,
I do not consider *hamrammr* to have its primary signification of actual transformation, but simply to mean subject to fits of diabolical possession, under the influence
of which the bodily powers were greatly exaggerated. I
shall translate pretty freely from this most interesting
Saga, as I consider that the description given in it
of Kveldulf in his fits greatly elucidates our subject.

" Kveldulf and Skallagrim got news during summer

of an expedition. Skallagrim was the keenest-sighted of men, and he caught sight of the vessel of Hallvard and his brother, and recognized it at once. He followed their course and marked the haven into which they entered at even. Then he returned to his company, and told Kveldulf of what he had seen . . . . Then they busked them and got ready both their boats; in each they put twenty men, Kveldulf steering one and Skallagrim the other, and they rowed in quest of the ship. Now when they came to the place where it was, they lay to. Hallvard and his men had spread an awning over the deck, and were asleep. Now when Kveldulf and his party came upon them, the watchers who were seated at the end of the bridge sprang up and called to the people on board to wake up, for there was danger in the wind. So Hallvard and his men sprang to arms. Then came Kveldulf over the bridge and Skallagrim with him into the ship. Kveldulf had in his hand a cleaver, and he bade his men go through the vessel and hack away the awning. But he pressed on to the quarter-deck. It is said the were-wolf fit came over him and many of his companions. They slew all the men who were before them. Skallagrim did the same as he went round the vessel. He and his father paused not till they had cleared it. Now when Kveldulf came upon the quarter-deck he raised his cleaver, and smote Hallvard through helm and head, so that the haft was buried in the flesh; but he dragged it to him so violently that he whisked Hallvard into the air, and flung him overboard. Skallagrim cleared the forecastle and slew Sigtrygg. Many men flung themselves overboard, but Skallagrim's men took to the boat and rowed about, killing all they found. Thus perished Hallvard with fifty men. Skallagrim and his party took the ship and all the goods which had belonged to Hallvard . . . and flitted it and the wares to their own vessel, and then exchanged ships, lading their capture, but quitting their own. After which they filled their old ship with stones, brake it up and sank it. A good breeze sprang up, and they stood out to sea.

"It is said of these men in the engagement who were were-wolves, or those on whom came the berserkr rage, that as long as the fit was on them no one could oppose them, they were so strong; but when it had passed off they were feebler than usual. It was the same with Kveldulf when the were-wolf fit went off him—he then felt the exhaustion consequent on the fight, and he was so completely 'done up,' that he was obliged to take to his bed."

In like manner Skallagrim had his fits of frenzy, taking after his amiable father.

" Thord and his companion were opposed to Skallagrim in the game, and they were too much for him, he wearied, and the game went better with them. But at dusk, after sunset, it went worse with Egill and Thord, for Skallagrim became so strong that he caught up Thord and cast him down, so that he broke his bones, and that was the death of him. Then he caught at Egill. Thorgerd Brák was the name of a servant of Skallagrim, who had been foster-mother to Egill. She was a woman of great stature, strong as a man and a bit of a witch. Brák exclaimed,—' Skallagrim! are you now falling upon your son ? ' (hamaz þú at syni þínum). Then Skallagrim let go his hold of Egill and clutched at her. She started aside and fled. Skallagrim followed. They ran out upon Digraness, and she sprang off the headland into the water. Skallagrim cast after her a huge stone which struck her between the shoulders, and she never rose after it. The place is now called Brak's Sound."—(c. 40.)

Let it be observed that in these passages from the *Aigla*, the words aꝛ hamaz, hamrammr, &c. are used without any intention of conveying the idea of a change

of bodily shape, though the words taken literally assert
it.   For they are derived from *hamr*, a skin or habit; a
word which has its representatives in other Aryan
languages, and is therefore a primitive word expressive
of the skin of a beast.

The Sanskrit चर्म्म *carmma;* the Hindustanee چام
câm, hide or skin; and چمرا *camra,* leather; the
Persian حامه *ǧame,* clothing, disguise; the Gothic
ham or *hams,* skin; and even the Italian *camicia,*
and the French *chemise,* are cognate words.*

It seems probable accordingly that the verb að *hamaz*
was first applied to those who wore the skins of savage
animals, and went about the country as freebooters; but
that popular superstition soon invested them with
supernatural powers, and they were supposed to assume
the forms of the beasts in whose skins they were dis-
guised.   The verb then acquired the significance "to
become a were-wolf, to change shape."   It did not stop
there, but went through another change of meaning,
and was finally applied to those who were afflicted
with paroxysms of madness or demoniacal possession.

This was not the only word connected with were-

---

* I shall have more to say on this subject in the chapter on the
Mythology of Lycanthropy.

wolves which helped on the superstition. The word
vargr, a wolf, had a double significance, which would
be the means of originating many a were-wolf story.
Vargr is the same as *u-argr*, restless; *argr* being the
same as the Anglo-Saxon *earg*. *Vargr* had its double
signification in Norse. It signified a wolf, and also a
godless man. This *vargr* is the English *were*, in the
word were-wolf, and the *garou* or *varou* in French. The
Danish word for were-wolf is *var-ulf*, the Gothic *vaira-
ulf*. In the *Romans de Garin*, it is "Leu warou,
sanglante beste." In the *Vie de S. Hildefons* by Gauthier
de Coinsi,—

> Cil lou desve, cil lou garol,
> Ce sunt deable, que saul
> Ne puent estre de nos mordre.

Here the loup-garou is a devil. The Anglo-Saxons
regarded him as an evil man: *wearg*, a scoundrel;
Gothic *vargs*, a fiend. But very often the word meant no
more than an outlaw. Pluquet in his *Contes Populaires*
tells us that the ancient Norman laws said of the
criminals condemned to outlawry for certain offences,
Wargus esto: be an outlaw!

In like manner the Lex Ripuaria, tit. 87, "Wargus
sit, hoc est expulsus." In the laws of Canute, he is
called verevulf. (*Leges Canuti*, Schmid, i. 148.) And

the Salic Law (tit. 57) orders : " Si quis corpus jam sepultum effoderit, aut expoliaverit, *wargus* sit." " If any one shall have dug up or despoiled an already buried corpse, let him be a varg."

Sidonius Apollinaris says, " Unam feminam quam forte *vargorum,* hoc enim nomine indigenas latrunculos nuncupant,"* as though the common name by which those who lived a freebooter life were designated, was varg.

In like manner Palgrave assures us in his *Rise and Progress of the English Commonwealth,* that among the Anglo Saxons an *utlagh,* or out-law, was said to have the head of a wolf. If then the term *vargr* was applied at one time to a wolf, at another to an outlaw who lived the life of a wild beast, away from the haunts of men— "he shall be driven away as a wolf, and chased so far as men chase wolves farthest," was the legal form of sentence—it is certainly no matter of wonder that stories of out-laws should have become surrounded with mythical accounts of their transformation into wolves.

But the very idiom of the Norse was calculated to foster this superstition. The Icelanders had curious expressions which are sufficiently likely to have produced misconceptions.

---

* SIDONIUS APOLLINARIS : *Opera,* lib. vi. ep. 4.

Snorri not only relates that Odin changed himself into another form, but he adds that by his spells he turned his enemies into boars. In precisely the same manner does a hag, Ljot, in the Vatnsdæla Saga, say that she could have turned Thorsteinn and Jökull into boars to run about with the wild beasts (c. xxvi.) ; and the expression *verða at gjalti*, or *at gjöltum*, to become a boar, is frequently met with in the Sagas.

" Thereupon came Thorarinn and his men upon them, and Nagli led the way ; but when he saw weapons drawn he was frightened, and ran away up the mountain, and became a boar. . . . And Thorarinn and his men took to run, so as to help Nagli, lest he should tumble off the cliffs into the sea " (Eyrbyggja Saga, c. xviii.) A similar expression occurs in the Gisla Saga Surssonar, p. 50. In the Hrolfs Saga Kraka, we meet with a troll in boar's shape, to whom divine honours are paid ; and in the Kjalnessinga Saga, c. xv., men are likened to boars—" Then it began to fare with them as it fares with boars when they fight each other, for in the same manner dropped their foam." The true significa- tion of *verða at gjalti* is to be in such a state of fear as to lose the senses ; but it is sufficiently peculiar to have given rise to superstitious stories.

I have dwelt at some length on the Northern myths relative to were-wolves and animal transformations, because I have considered the investigation of these all-important towards the elucidation of the truth which lies at the bottom of mediæval superstition, and which is nowhere so obtainable as through the Norse literature. As may be seen from the passages quoted above at length, and from an examination of those merely referred to, the result arrived at is pretty conclusive, and may be summed up in very few words.

The whole superstructure of fable and romance relative to transformation into wild beasts, reposes simply on this basis of truth—that among the Scandinavian nations there existed a form of madness or possession, under the influence of which men acted as though they were changed into wild and savage brutes, howling, foaming at the mouth, ravening for blood and slaughter, ready to commit any act of atrocity, and as irresponsible for their actions as the wolves and bears, in whose skins they often equipped themselves.

The manner in which this fact became invested with supernatural adjuncts I have also pointed out, to wit, the change in the significance of the word designating the madness, the double meaning of the word *vargr*, and above all, the habits and appearance of the maniacs. We shall see instances of berserkr rage reappearing in the middle ages, and late down into our own times, not exclusively in the North, but throughout France, Germany, and England, and instead of rejecting the accounts given by chroniclers as fabulous, because there is much connected with them which seems to be fabulous, we shall be able to refer them to their true origin.

It may be accepted as an axiom, that no superstition of general acceptance is destitute of a foundation of truth; and if we discover the myth of the were-wolf to be widely spread, not only throughout Europe, but through the whole world, we may rest assured that there is a solid core of fact, round which popular superstition has crystallized; and that fact is the existence of a species of madness, during the accesses of which the person afflicted believes himself to be a wild beast, and acts like a wild beast.

In some cases this madness amounts apparently to positive possession, and the diabolical acts into which the possessed is impelled are so horrible, that the blood curdles in reading them, and it is impossible to recall them without a shudder.

CHAPTER V.

THE WERE-WOLF IN THE MIDDLE-AGES.

Stories from Olaus Magnus of Livonian Were-wolves—Story from Bishop Majolus—Story of Albertus Pericofcius—Similar occurrence at Prague—Saint Patrick—Strange incident related by John of Nüremberg—Bisclaveret—Courland Were-wolves—Pierre Vidal—Pavian Lycanthropist—Bodin's Stories—Forestus' account of a Lycanthropist—Neapolitan Were-wolf.

OLAUS MAGNUS relates that—"In Prussia, Livonia, and Lithuania, although the inhabitants suffer considerably from the rapacity of wolves throughout the year, in that these animals rend their cattle, which are scattered in great numbers through the woods, whenever they stray in the very least, yet this is not regarded by them as such a serious matter as what they endure from men turned into wolves.

"On the feast of the Nativity of Christ, at night, such a multitude of wolves transformed from men gather together in a certain spot, arranged among themselves,

and then spread to rage with wondrous ferocity against
human beings, and those animals which are not wild,
that the natives of these regions suffer more detriment
from these, than they do from true and natural wolves ;
for when a human habitation has been detected by them
isolated in the woods, they besiege it with atrocity,
striving to break in the doors, and in the event of their
doing so, they devour all the human beings, and every
animal which is found within. They burst into the beer-
cellars, and there they empty the tuns of beer or mead,
and pile up the empty casks one above another in the
middle of the cellar, thus showing their difference from
natural and genuine wolves. . . . Between Lithuania,
Livonia, and Courland are the walls of a certain
old ruined castle. At this spot congregate thousands,
on a fixed occasion, and try their agility in jumping.
Those who are unable to bound over the wall, as is often
the case with the fattest, are fallen upon with scourges by
the captains and slain." * Olaus relates also in c. xlvii.
the story of a certain nobleman who was travelling
through a large forest with some peasants in his retinue
who dabbled in the black art. They found no house

---

* OLAUS MAGNUS : *Historia de Vent. Septent.* Basil. 15, lib. xviii.
cap. 45.

where they could lodge for the night, and were well-nigh famished. Then one of the peasants offered, if all the rest would hold their tongues as to what he should do, that he would bring them a lamb from a distant flock.

He thereupon retired into the depths of the forest and changed his form into that of a wolf, fell upon the flock, and brought a lamb to his companions in his mouth. They received it with gratitude. Then he retired once more into the thicket, and transformed himself back again into his human shape.

The wife of a nobleman in Livonia expressed her doubts to one of her slaves whether it were possible for man or woman thus to change shape. The servant at once volunteered to give her evidence of the possibility. He left the room, and in another moment a wolf was observed running over the country. The dogs followed him, and notwithstanding his resistance, tore out one of his eyes. Next day the slave appeared before his mistress blind of an eye.

Bp. Majolus * and Caspar Peucer† relate the following circumstances of the Livonians :—

---

* MAJOLI *Episc. Vulturoniensis Dier. Canicul.* Helenopolis, 1612, tom. ii. colloq. 3.

† CASPAR PEUCER : *Comment. de Præcipuis Divin. Generibus,* 1591, p. 169.

At Christmas a boy lame of a leg goes round the country summoning the devil's followers, who are countless, to a general conclave. Whoever remains behind, or goes reluctantly, is scourged by another with an iron whip till the blood flows, and his traces are left in blood. The human form vanishes, and the whole multitude become wolves. Many thousands assemble. Foremost goes the leader armed with an iron whip, and the troop follow, "firmly convinced in their imaginations that they are transformed into wolves." They fall upon herds of cattle and flocks of sheep, but they have no power to slay men. When they come to a river, the leader smites the water with his scourge, and it divides, leaving a dry path through the midst, by which the pack may go. The transformation lasts during twelve days, at the expiration of which period the wolf-skin vanishes, and the human form reappears. This superstition was expressly forbidden by the church. " Credidisti, quod quidam credere solent, ut illæ quæ a vulgo Parcæ vocantur, ipsæ vel sint vel possint hoc facere quod creduntur, id est, dum aliquis homo nascitur, et tunc valeant illum designare ad hoc quod velint, ut quandocunque homo ille voluerit, in lupum transformari possit, quod vulgaris stultitia *werwolf* vocat, aut in aliam aliquam figuram?" — Ap. Burchard (d. 1024). In like manner did S. Boniface preach against those who believed superstitiously in "strigas et fictos lupos." (*Serm.* apud Mart. et Durand. ix. 217.)

In a dissertation by Müller * we learn, on the authority of Cluverius and Dannhaverus (*Acad. Homilet.* p. ii.), that a certain Albertus Pericofcius in Muscovy was wont to tyrannize over and harass his subjects in the most unscrupulous manner. One night when he was absent from home, his whole herd of cattle, acquired by extortion, perished. On his return he was informed of his loss, and the wicked man broke out into the most horrible blasphemies, exclaiming, "Let him who has slain, eat; if God chooses, let him devour me as well."

As he spoke, drops of blood fell to earth, and the nobleman, transformed into a wild dog, rushed upon his dead cattle, tore and mangled the carcasses and began to devour them; possibly he may be devouring them still (*ac forsan hodieque pascitur*). His wife, then near her confinement, died of fear. Of these circumstances there were not only ear but also eye witnesses. (*Non ab auritis tantum, sed et oculatis accepi, quod*

---

* *De* Λυκανθρωπία. Lipsiæ, 1736.

narro). Similarly it is related of a nobleman in the neighbourhood of Prague, that he robbed his subjects of their goods and reduced them to penury through his exactions. He took the last cow from a poor widow with five children, but as a judgment, all his own cattle died. He then broke into fearful oaths, and God transformed him into a dog: his human head, however, remained.

S. Patrick is said to have changed Vereticus, king of Wales, into a wolf, and S. Natalis, the abbot, to have pronounced anathema upon an illustrious family in Ireland; in consequence of which, every male and female take the form of wolves for seven years and live in the forests and career over the bogs, howling mournfully, and appeasing their hunger upon the sheep of the peasants.* A duke of Prussia, according to Majolus, had a countryman brought for sentence before him, because he had devoured his neighbour's cattle. The fellow was an ill-favoured, deformed man, with great wounds in his face, which he had received from dogs' bites whilst he had been in his wolf's form. It was believed that he changed shape twice in the year, at Christmas and at Midsummer. He was said to exhibit much uneasiness

* PHIL. HARTUNG : *Conciones Tergeminæ*, pars ii. p. 367.

and discomfort when the wolf-hair began to break out and his bodily shape to change.

He was kept long in prison and closely watched, lest he should become a were-wolf during his confinement and attempt to escape, but nothing remarkable took place. If this is the same individual as that mentioned by Olaus Magnus, as there seems to be a probability, the poor fellow was burned alive.

John of Nüremberg relates the following curious story.[*] A priest was once travelling in a strange country, and lost his way in a forest. Seeing a fire, he made towards it, and beheld a wolf seated over it. The wolf addressed him in human voice, and bade him not fear, as " he was of the Ossyrian race, of which a man and a woman were doomed to spend a certain number of years in wolf's form. Only after seven years might they return home and resume their former shapes, if thcy were still alive." He begged the priest to visit and console his sick wife, and to give her the last sacraments. This the priest consented to do, after some hesitation, and only when convinced of the beasts being human beings, by observing that the wolf used his front paws as hands, and when he saw the

---

[*] JOHN EUS. NIERENBERG *de Miracul. in Europa*, lib. ii. cap. 42.

she-wolf peel off her wolf-skin from her head to her navel, exhibiting the features of an aged woman.

Marie de France says in the *Lais du Bisclaveret :*—*

> Bisclaveret ad nun en Bretan
> Garwall l'apelent li Norman.
> *   *   *   *
> Jadis le poet-hum oir
> Et souvent suleit avenir,
> Humes pluseirs Garwall deviendrent
> E es boscages meisun tindrent.

There is an interesting paper by Rhanæus, on the Courland were-wolves, in the *Breslauer Sammlung.†* The author says,—" There are too many examples derived not merely from hearsay, but received on indisputable evidence, for us to dispute the fact, that Satan —if we do not deny that such a being exists, and that he has his work in the children of darkness—holds the Lycanthropists in his net in three ways :—

" 1. They execute as wolves certain acts, such as seizing a sheep, or destroying cattle, &c., not changed into wolves, which no scientific man in Courland believes, but in their human frames, and with their

---

* An epitome of this curious were-wolf tale will be found in Ellis's *Early English Metrical Romances.*

† Supplement III. *Curieuser* und nutzbarer Anmerkungen von Natur und Kunstgeschichten, gesammelt von Kanold. 1728.

human limbs, yet in such a state of phantasy and hallucination, that they believe themselves transformed into wolves, and are regarded as such by others suffering under similar hallucination, and in this manner run these people in packs as wolves, though not true wolves.

"2. They imagine, in deep sleep or dream, that they injure the cattle, and this without leaving their couch; but it is their master who does, in their stead, what their fancy points out, or suggests to him.

"3. The evil one drives natural wolves to do some act, and then pictures it so well to the sleeper, immovable in his place, both in dreams and at awaking, that he believes the act to have been committed by himself."

Rhanæus, under these heads, relates three stories, which he believes he has on good authority. The first is of a gentleman starting on a journey, who came upon a wolf engaged in the act of seizing a sheep in his own flock; he fired at it, and wounded it, so that it fled howling to the thicket. When the gentleman returned from his expedition he found the whole neighbourhood impressed with the belief that he had, on a given day and hour, shot at one of his tenants, a publican, Mickel.

On inquiry, the man's wife, called Lebba, related the following circumstances, which were fully corroborated by numerous witnesses :—When her husband had sown his rye he had consulted with his wife how he was to get some meat, so as to have a good feast. The woman urged him on no account to steal from his landlord's flock, because it was guarded by fierce dogs. He, however, rejected her advice, and Mickel fell upon his landlord's sheep, but he had suffered and had come limping home, and in his rage at the ill success of his attempt, had fallen upon his own horse and had bitten its throat completely through. This took place in the year 1684.

In 1684, a man was about to fire upon a pack of wolves, when he heard from among the troop a voice exclaiming—" Gossip ! Gossip ! don't fire. No good will come of it."

The third story is as follows :—A lycanthropist was brought before a judge and accused of witchcraft, but as nothing could be proved against him, the judge ordered one of his peasants to visit the man in his prison, and to worm the truth out of him, and to persuade the prisoner to assist him in revenging himself upon another peasant who had injured him; and this

was to be effected by destroying one of the man's cows;
but the peasant was to urge the prisoner to do it
secretly, and, if possible, in the disguise of a wolf.
The fellow undertook the task, but he had great difficulty in persuading the prisoner to fall in with his
wishes: eventually, however, he succeeded. Next morning
the cow was found in its stall frightfully mangled, but the
prisoner had not left his cell: for the watch, who had
been placed to observe him, declared that he had spent
the night in profound sleep, and that he had only at
one time made a slight motion with his head and hands
and feet.

Wierius and Forestus quote Gulielmus Brabantinus
as an authority for the fact, that a man of high position had been so possessed by the evil one, that often
during the year he fell into a condition in which he
believed himself to be turned into a wolf, and at that
time he roved in the woods and tried to seize and
devour little children, but that at last, by God's mercy,
he recovered his senses.

Certainly the famous Pierre Vidal, the Don Quixote
of Provençal troubadours, must have had a touch of this
madness, when, after having fallen in love with a lady
of Carcassone, named Loba, or the Wolfess, the excess

of his passion drove him over the country, howling like
a wolf, and demeaning himself more like an irrational
beast than a rational man.

He commemorates his lupine madness in the poem
A tal Donna :—*

> Crowned with immortal joys I mount
> The proudest emperors above,
> For I am honoured with the love
> Of the fair daughter of a count.
> A lace from Na Raymbauda's hand
> I value more than all the land
> Of Richard, with his Poïctou,
> His rich Touraine and famed Anjou.
>   When *loup-garou* the rabble call me,
> When vagrant shepherds hoot,
> Pursue, and buffet me to boot,
> It doth not for a moment gall me;
> I seek not palaces or halls,
> Or refuge when the winter falls;
> Exposed to winds and frosts at night,
> My soul is ravished with delight.
>   Me claims my she-wolf (*Loba*) so divine:
> And justly she that claim prefers,
> For, by my troth, my life is hers
> More than another's, more than mine.

Job Fincelius † relates the sad story of a farmer of
Pavia, who, as a wolf, fell upon many men in the open
country and tore them to pieces. After much trouble

---

* BRUCE WHYTE: *Histoire des Langues Romaines*, tom. ii. p. 248.
† FINCELIUS *de Mirabilibus*, lib. xi.

the maniac was caught, and he then assured his captors that the only difference which existed between himself and a natural wolf, was that in a true wolf the hair grew outward, whilst in him it struck inward. In order to put this assertion to the proof, the magistrates, themselves most certainly cruel and bloodthirsty wolves, cut off his arms and legs; the poor wretch died of the mutilation. This took place in 1541. The idea of the skin being reversed is a very ancient one : *versipellis* occurs as a name of reproach in Petronius, Lucilius, and Plautus, and resembles the Norse *hamrammr*.

Fincelius relates also that, in 1542, there was such a multitude of were-wolves about Constantinople that the Emperor, accompanied by his guard, left the city to give them a severe correction, and slew one hundred and fifty of them.

Spranger speaks of three young ladies who attacked a labourer, under the form of cats, and were wounded by him. They were found bleeding in their beds next morning.

Majolus relates that a man afflicted with lycanthropy was brought to Pomponatius. The poor fellow had been found buried in hay, and when people approached, he called to them to flee, as he was a were-

wolf, and would rend them. The country-folk wanted
to flay him, to discover whether the hair grew inwards,
but Pomponatius rescued the man and cured him.

Bodin tells some were-wolf stories on good authority;
it is a pity that the good authorities of Bodin were such
liars, but that, by the way. He says that the Royal
Procurator-General Bourdin had assured him that he
had shot a wolf, and that the arrow had stuck in the
beast's thigh. A few hours after, the arrow was found
in the thigh of a man in bed. In Vernon, about the
year 1566, the witches and warlocks gathered in great
multitudes, under the shape of cats. Four or five men
were attacked in a lone place by a number of these
beasts. The men stood their ground with the utmost
heroism, succeeded in slaying one puss, and in wounding
many others. Next day a number of wounded women
were found in the town, and they gave the judge an
accurate account of all the circumstances connected with
their wounding.

Bodin quotes Pierre Marner, the author of a treatise
on sorcerers, as having witnessed in Savoy the transformation of men into wolves. Nynauld * relates that
in a village of Switzerland, near Lucerne, a peasant was

---

* NYNAULD, *De la Lycanthropie.* Paris, 1615, p. 52.

attacked by a wolf, whilst he was hewing timber; he defended himself, and smote off a fore-leg of the beast. The moment that the blood began to flow the wolf's form changed, and he recognized a woman without her arm. She was burnt alive.

An evidence that beasts are transformed witches is to be found in their having no tails. When the devil takes human form, however, he keeps his club-foot of the Satyr, as a token by which he may be recognized. So animals deficient in caudal appendages are to be avoided, as they are witches in disguise. The Thingwald should consider the case of the Manx cats in its next session.

Forestus, in his chapter on maladies of the brain, relates a circumstance which came under his own observation, in the middle of the sixteenth century, at Alcmaar in the Netherlands. A peasant there was attacked every spring with a fit of insanity; under the influence of this he rushed about the churchyard, ran into the church, jumped over the benches, danced, was filled with fury, climbed up, descended, and never remained quiet. He carried a long staff in his hand, with which he drove away the dogs, which flew at him and wounded him, so that his thighs were covered with scars. His face was pale, his eyes deep sunk in their sockets.   Forestus pronounces the man to be a lycanthropist, but he does not say that the poor fellow believed himself to be transformed into a wolf. In reference to this case, however, he mentions that of a Spanish nobleman who believed himself to be changed into a bear, and who wandered filled with fury among the woods.

Donatus of Altomare * affirms that he saw a man in the streets of Naples, surrounded by a ring of people, who in his were-wolf frenzy had dug up a corpse and was carrying off the leg upon his shoulders.   This was in the middle of the sixteenth century.

---

* *De Medend. Human. Corp.* lib. i. cap. 9.

CHAPTER VI.

A CHAPTER OF HORRORS.

Pierre Bourgot and Michel Verdung—The Hermit of S. Bonnot—The Gandillon Family—Thievenne Paget—The Tailor of Châlons—Roulet.

IN December, 1521, the Inquisitor-General for the diocese of Besançon, Boin by name, heard a case of a sufficiently terrible nature to produce a profound sensation of alarm in the neighbourhood. Two men were under accusation of witchcraft and cannibalism. Their names were Pierre Bourgot, or Peter the Great, as the people had nicknamed him from his stature, and Michel Verdung. Peter had not been long under trial, before he volunteered a full confession of his crimes. It amounted to this :—

About nineteen years before, on the occasion of a New Year's market at Poligny, a terrible storm had broken over the country, and among other mischiefs done by it, was the scattering of Pierre's flock. "In vain," said the prisoner, "did I labour, in company with other peasants, to find the sheep and bring them together. I went everywhere in search of them.

"Then there rode up three black horsemen, and the last said to me: 'Whither away? you seem to be in trouble?'

"I related to him my misfortune with my flock. He bade me pluck up my spirits, and promised that his master would henceforth take charge of and protect my flock, if I would only rely upon him. He told me, as well, that I should find my strayed sheep very shortly, and he promised to provide me with money. We agreed to meet again in four or five days. My flock I soon found collected together. At my second meeting I learned of the stranger that he was a servant of the devil. I forswore God and our Lady and all saints and dwellers in Paradise. I renounced Christianity, kissed his left hand, which was black and ice-cold as that of a corpse. Then I fell on my knees and gave in my allegiance to Satan. I remained in the service of the devil for two years, and never entered a church before the end of mass, or at all events till the holy water had been sprinkled, according to the desire of my master, whose name I afterwards learned was Moyset.

" All anxiety about my flock was removed, for the devil had undertaken to protect it and to keep off the wolves.

" This freedom from care, however, made me begin to tire of the devil's service, and I recommenced my attendance at church, till I was brought back into obedience to the evil one by Michel Verdung, when I renewed my compact on the understanding that I should be supplied with money.

" In a wood near Chastel Charnon we met with many others whom I did not recognize ; we danced, and each had in his or her hand a green taper with a blue flame. Still under the delusion that I should obtain money, Michel persuaded me to move with the greatest celerity, and in order to do this, after I had stripped myself, he smeared me with a salve, and I believed myself then to be transformed into a wolf. I was at first somewhat horrified at my four wolf's feet, and the fur with which I was covered all at once, but I found that I could now travel with the speed of the wind. This could not have taken place without the help of our powerful master, who was present during our excursion, though I did not perceive him till I had recovered my human form. Michel did the same as myself.

"When we had been one or two hours in this condition of metamorphosis, Michel smeared us again, and quick as thought we resumed our human forms. The salve was given us by our masters; to me it was given by Moyset, to Michel by his own master, Guillemin."

Pierre declared that he felt no exhaustion after his excursions, though the judge inquired particularly whether he felt that prostration after his unusual exertion, of which witches usually complained. Indeed the exhaustion consequent on a were-wolf raid was so great that the lycanthropist was often confined to his bed for days, and could hardly move hand or foot, much in the same way as the *berserkir* and *ham rammir* in the North were utterly prostrated after their fit had left them.

In one of his were-wolf runs, Pierre fell upon a boy of six or seven years old, with his teeth, intending to rend and devour him, but the lad screamed so loud that he was obliged to beat a retreat to his clothes, and smear himself again, in order to recover his form and escape detection. He and Michel, however, one day tore to pieces a woman as she was gathering peas; and a M. de Chusnée, who came to her rescue, was attacked by them and killed.

On another occasion they fell upon a little girl of four years old, and ate her up, with the exception of one arm. Michel thought the flesh most delicious.

Another girl was strangled by them, and her blood lapped up. Of a third they ate merely a portion of the stomach. One evening at dusk, Pierre leaped over a garden wall, and came upon a little maiden of nine years old, engaged upon the weeding of the garden beds. She fell on her knees and entreated Pierre to spare her; but he snapped the neck, and left her a corpse, lying among her flowers. On this occasion he does not seem to have been in his wolf's shape. He fell upon a goat which he found in the field of Pierre Lerugen, and bit it in the throat, but he killed it with a knife.

Michel was transformed in his clothes into a wolf, but Pierre was obliged to strip, and the metamorphosis could not take place with him unless he were stark naked.

He was unable to account for the manner in which the hair vanished when he recovered his natural condition.

The statements of Pierre Bourgot were fully corroborated by Michel Verdung.

Towards the close of the autumn of 1573, the peasants of the neighbourhood of Dôle, in Franche Comté, were authorized by the Court of Parliament at Dôle, to hunt down the were-wolves which infested the country. The authorization was as follows :—" According to the advertisement made to the sovereign Court of Parliament at Dôle, that, in the territories of Espagny, Salvange, Courchapon, and the neighbouring villages, has often been seen and met, for some time past, a were-wolf, who, it is said, has already seized and carried off several little children, so that they have not been seen since, and since he has attacked and done injury in the country to some horsemen, who kept him off only with great difficulty and danger to their persons : the said Court, desiring to prevent any greater danger, has permitted, and does permit, those who are abiding or dwelling in the said places and others, notwithstanding all edicts concerning the chase, to assemble with pikes, halberts, arquebuses, and sticks, to chase and to pursue the said were-wolf in every place where they may find or seize him ; to tie and to kill, without incurring any pains or penalties. . . . Given at the meeting of the said Court, on the thirteenth day of the month September, 1573." It was some time, however, before the loup-garou was caught.

In a retired spot near Amanges, half shrouded in trees, stood a small hovel of the rudest construction; its roof was of turf, and its walls were blotched with lichen. The garden to this cot was run to waste, and the fence round it broken through. As the hovel was far from any road, and was only reached by a path over moorland and through forest, it was seldom visited, and the couple who lived in it were not such as would make many friends. The man, Gilles Garnier, was a sombre, ill-looking fellow, who walked in a stooping attitude, and whose pale face, livid complexion, and deep-set eyes under a pair of coarse and bushy brows, which met across the forehead, were sufficient to repel any one from seeking his acquaintance. Gilles seldom spoke, and when he did it was in the broadest patois of his country. His long grey beard and retiring habits procured for him the name of the Hermit of St. Bonnot, though no one for a moment attributed to him any extraordinary amount of sanctity.

The hermit does not seem to have been suspected for some time, but one day, as some of the peasants of

Chastenoy were returning home from their work, through the forest, the screams of a child and the deep baying of a wolf, attracted their notice, and on running in the direction whence the cries sounded, they found a little girl defending herself against a monstrous creature, which was attacking her tooth and nail, and had already wounded her severely in five places. As the peasants came up, the creature fled on all fours into the gloom of the thicket; it was so dark that it could not be identified with certainty, and whilst some affirmed that it was a wolf, others thought they had recognized the features of the hermit. This took place on the 8th November.

On the 14th a little boy of ten years old was missing, who had been last seen at a short distance from the gates of Dôle.

The hermit of S. Bonnot was now seized and brought to trial at Dôle, when the following evidence was extracted from him and his wife, and substantiated in many particulars by witnesses.

On the last day of Michaelmas, under the form of a wolf, at a mile from Dôle, in the farm of Gorge, a vineyard belonging to Chastenoy, near the wood of La Serre, Gilles Garnier had attacked a little maiden of ten or twelve years old, and had slain her with his teeth and claws; he had then drawn her into the wood, stripped her, gnawed the flesh from her legs and arms, and had enjoyed his meal so much, that, inspired with conjugal affection, he had brought some of the flesh home for his wife Apolline.

Eight days after the feast of All Saints, again in the form of a were-wolf, he had seized another girl, near the meadow land of La Pouppe, on the territory of Athume and Chastenoy, and was on the point of slaying and devouring her, when three persons came up, and he was compelled to escape. On the fourteenth day after All Saints, also as a wolf, he had attacked a boy of ten years old, a mile from Dôle, between Gredisans and Menoté, and had strangled him. On that occasion he had eaten all the flesh off his legs and arms, and had also devoured a great part of the belly; one of the legs he had rent completely from the trunk with his fangs.

On the Friday before the last feast of S. Bartholomew, he had seized a boy of twelve or thirteen, under a large pear-tree near the wood of the village Perrouze, and had drawn him into the thicket and killed him, intending to eat him as he had eaten the other children, but the approach of men hindered him from fulfilling his intention. The boy was, however, quite dead, and the men who came up declared that Gilles appeared as a man and not as a wolf. The hermit of S. Bonnot was sentenced to be dragged to the place of public execution, and there to be burned alive, a sentence which was rigorously carried out.

In this instance the poor maniac fully believed that actual transformation into a wolf took place; he was apparently perfectly reasonable on other points, and quite conscious of the acts he had committed.

We come now to a more remarkable circumstance, the affliction of a whole family with the same form of insanity. Our information is derived from Boguet's *Discours de Sorciers*, 1603—1610.

Pernette Gandillon was a poor girl in the Jura, who in 1598 ran about the country on all fours, in the belief that she was a wolf. One day as she was ranging the country in a fit of lycanthropic madness, she came upon two children who were plucking wild strawberries. Filled with a sudden passion for blood, she flew at the little girl and would have brought her down, had not her brother, a lad of four years old, defended her lustily with a knife. Pernette, however, wrenched the weapon from his tiny hand, flung him down and gashed his throat, so that he died of the wound. Pernette was torn to pieces by the people in their rage and horror.

Directly after, Pierre, the brother of Pernette Gandillon, was accused of witchcraft. He was charged with having led children to the sabbath, having made hail, and having run about the country in the form of a wolf. The transformation was effected by means of a salve which he had received from the devil. He had on one occasion assumed the form of a hare, but usually he appeared as a wolf, and his skin became covered with shaggy grey hair. He readily acknowledged that the charges brought against him were well founded, and he allowed that he had, during the period of his transformation, fallen on, and devoured, both beasts and human beings. When he desired to recover his true form, he rolled himself in the dewy grass. His son Georges asserted that he had also been anointed with the salve, and had gone to the sabbath in the shape of a wolf. According to his own testimony, he had fallen upon two goats in one of his expeditions.

One Maundy-Thursday night he had lain for three hours in his bed in a cataleptic state, and at the end of that time had sprung out of bed. During this period he had been in the form of a wolf to the witches' sabbath.

His sister Antoinnette confessed that she had made hail, and that she had sold herself to the devil, who had appeared to her in the shape of a black he-goat. She had been to the sabbath on several occasions.

Pierre and Georges in prison behaved as maniacs, running on all fours about their cells and howling dismally. Their faces, arms, and legs were frightfully scarred with the wounds they had received from dogs when they had been on their raids. Boguet accounts for the transformation not taking place, by the fact of their not having the necessary salves by them.

All three, Pierre, Georges, and Antoinnette, were hung and burned.

Thievenne Paget, who was a witch of the most unmistakable character, was also frequently changed into a she-wolf, according to her own confession, in which state she had often accompanied the devil over hill and dale, slaying cattle, and falling on and devouring children. The same thing may be said of Clauda Isan Prost, a lame woman, Clauda Isan Guillaume, and Isan Roquet, who owned to the murder of five children.

On the 14th of December, in the same year as the execution of the Gandillon family (1598), a tailor of Châlons was sentenced to the flames by the Parliament of Paris for lycanthropy. This wretched man had decoyed children into his shop, or attacked them in the gloaming when they strayed in the woods, had torn them with his teeth, and killed them, after which he seems calmly to have dressed their flesh as ordinary meat, and to have eaten it with great relish. The number of little innocents whom he destroyed is unknown. A whole cask full of bones was discovered in his house. The man was perfectly hardened, and the details of his trial were so full of horrors and abominations of all kinds, that the judges ordered the documents to be burned.

Again in 1598, a year memorable in the annals of lycanthropy, a trial took place in Angers, the details of which are very terrible.

In a wild and unfrequented spot near Caude, some countrymen came one day upon the corpse of a boy of fifteen, horribly mutilated and bespattered with blood. As the men approached, two wolves, which had been rending the body, bounded away into the thicket. The men gave chase immediately, following their bloody tracks till they lost them; when suddenly crouching among the bushes, his teeth chattering with fear, they found a man half naked, with long hair and beard, and with his hands dyed in blood. His nails were long as claws, and were clotted with fresh gore, and shreds of human flesh.

This is one of the most puzzling and peculiar cases which come under our notice.

The wretched man, whose name was Roulet, of his own accord stated that he had fallen upon the lad and had killed him by smothering him, and that he had been prevented from devouring the body completely by the arrival of men on the spot.

Roulet proved on investigation to be a beggar from house to house, in the most abject state of poverty. His companions in mendicity were his brother John and his cousin Julien. He had been given lodging out of charity in a neighbouring village, but before his apprehension he had been absent for eight days.

Before the judges, Roulet acknowledged that he was able to transform himself into a wolf by means of a salve which his parents had given him. When questioned about the two wolves which had been seen leaving the corpse, he said that he knew perfectly well who they were, for they were his companions, Jean and Julian, who possessed the same secret as himself. He was shown the clothes he had worn on the day of his seizure, and he recognized them immediately; he described the boy

whom he had murdered, gave the date correctly, indi-
cated the precise spot where the deed had been done,
and recognized the father of the boy as the man who
had first run up when the screams of the lad had been
heard. In prison, Roulet behaved like an idiot. When
seized, his belly was distended and hard; in prison he
drank one evening a whole pailful of water, and from
that moment refused to eat or drink.

His parents, on inquiry, proved to be respectable and
pious people, and they proved that his brother John and
his cousin Julien had been engaged at a distance on the
day of Roulet's apprehension.

"What is your name, and what your estate?" asked
the judge, Pierre Hérault.

"My name is Jacques Roulet, my age thirty-five; I
am poor, and a mendicant."

"What are you accused of having done?"

"Of being a thief—of having offended God. My
parents gave me an ointment; I do not know its composition."

"When rubbed with this ointment do you become
a wolf?"

"No; but for all that, I killed and ate the child
Cornier: I was a wolf."

" Were you dressed as a wolf ? "

" I was dressed as I am now. I had my hands and my face bloody, because I had been eating the flesh of the said child."

" Do your hands and feet become paws of a wolf ? "

" Yes, they do."

" Does your head become like that of a wolf—your mouth become larger ? "

" I do not know how my head was at the time ; I used my teeth ; my head was as it is to-day. I have wounded and eaten many other little children ; I have also been to the sabbath."

The *lieutenant criminel* sentenced Roulet to death. He, however, appealed to the Parliament at Paris ; and this decided that as there was more folly in the poor idiot than malice and witchcraft, his sentence of death should be commuted to two years' imprisonment in a madhouse, that he might be instructed in the knowledge of God, whom he had forgotten in his utter poverty.*

---

* " La cour du Parliament, par arrêt, mist l'appellation et la sentence dont il avoit esté appel au néant, et, néanmoins, ordonna que le dit Roulet serait mis à l'hospital Saint Germain des Prés, où on a accoustumé de mettre les folz, pour y demeurer l'espace de deux ans, afin d'y estre instruit et redressé tant de son esprit, que ramené à la cognoissance de Dieu, que l'extrême pauvreté lui avoit fait mescognoistre."

CHAPTER VII.

JEAN GRENIER.

On the Sand-dunes—A Wolf attacks Marguerite Poirier—Jean Grenier
brought to Trial—His Confessions—Charges of Cannibalism proved
—His Sentence—Behaviour in the Monastery—Visit of Del'ancre.

ONE fine afternoon in the spring, some village girls were
tending their sheep on the sand-dunes which intervene
between the vast forests of pine covering the greater
portion of the present department of *Landes* in the south
of France, and the sea.

The brightness of the sky, the freshness of the air
puffing up off the blue twinkling Bay of Biscay, the
hum or song of the wind as it made rich music among
the pines which stood like a green uplifted wave on the
East, the beauty of the sand-hills speckled with golden
cistus, or patched with gentian-blue, by the low growing
Gremille couchée, the charm of the forest-skirts, tinted

variously with the foliage of cork-trees, pines, and acacia, the latter in full bloom, a pile of rose-coloured or snowy flowers,—all conspired to fill the peasant maidens with joy, and to make their voices rise in song and laughter, which rung merrily over the hills, and through the dark avenues of evergreen trees.

Now a gorgeous butterfly attracted their attention, then a flight of quails skimming the surface.

" Ah! " exclaimed Jacquiline Auzun, " ah, if I had my stilts and bats, I would strike the little birds down, and we should have a fine supper."

" Now, if they would fly ready cooked into one's mouth, as they do in foreign parts!" said another girl.

" Have you got any new clothes for the S. Jean?" asked a third; " my mother has laid by to purchase me a smart cap with gold lace."

"You will turn the head of Etienne altogether, Annette!" said Jeanne Gaboriant. "But what is the matter with the sheep?"

She asked because the sheep which had been quietly browsing before her, on reaching a small depression in the *dune*, had started away as though frightened at something. At the same time one of the dogs began to growl and show his fangs.

The girls ran to the spot, and saw a little fall in the ground, in which, seated on a log of fir, was a boy of thirteen. The appearance of the lad was peculiar. His hair was of a tawny red and thickly matted, falling over his shoulders and completely covering his narrow brow. His small pale-grey eyes twinkled with an expression of horrible ferocity and cunning, from deep sunken hollows. The complexion was of a dark olive colour; the teeth were strong and white, and the canine teeth protruded over the lower lip when the mouth was closed. The boy's hands were large and powerful, the nails black and pointed like bird's talons. He was ill clothed, and seemed to be in the most abject poverty. The few garments he had on him were in tatters, and through the rents the emaciation of his limbs was plainly visible.

The girls stood round him, half frightened and much surprised, but the boy showed no symptoms of astonishment. His face relaxed into a ghastly leer, which showed the whole range of his glittering white fangs.

"Well, my maidens," said he in a harsh voice, "which of you is the prettiest, I should like to know; can you decide among you?"

"What do you want to know for?" asked Jeanne

Gaboriant, the eldest of the girls, aged eighteen, who took upon herself to be spokesman for the rest.

"Because I shall marry the prettiest," was the answer.

"Ah!" said Jeanne jokingly; "that is if she will have you, which is not very likely, as we none of us know you, or anything about you."

"I am the son of a priest," replied the boy curtly.

"Is that why you look so dingy and black?"

"No, I am dark-coloured, because I wear a wolf-skin sometimes."

"A wolf-skin!" echoed the girl; "and pray who gave it you?"

"One called Pierre Labourant."

"There is no man of that name hereabouts. Where does he live?"

A scream of laughter mingled with howls, and breaking into strange gulping bursts of fiendlike merriment from the strange boy.

The little girls recoiled, and the youngest took refuge behind Jeanne.

"Do you want to know Pierre Labourant, lass? Hey, he is a man with an iron chain about his neck, which he is ever engaged in gnawing. Do you want to know where he lives, lass? Ha, in a place of gloom and fire, where there are many companions, some seated on iron chairs, burning, burning; others stretched on glowing beds, burning too. Some cast men upon blazing coals, others roast men before fierce flames, others again plunge them into caldrons of liquid fire."

The girls trembled and looked at each other with scared faces, and then again at the hideous being which crouched before them.

"You want to know about the wolf-skin cape?" continued he. "Pierre Labourant gave me that; he wraps it round me, and every Monday, Friday, and Sunday, and for about an hour at dusk every other day, I am a wolf, a were-wolf. I have killed dogs and drunk their blood; but little girls taste better, their flesh is tender and sweet, their blood rich and warm. I have eaten many a maiden, as I have been on my raids together with my nine companions. I am a were-wolf! Ah, ha! if the sun were to set I would soon fall on one of you and make a meal of you!" Again he burst into one of his frightful paroxysms of laughter, and the girls unable to endure it any longer, fled with precipitation.

Near the village of S. Antoine de Pizon, a little girl of the name of Marguerite Poirier, thirteen years old, was in the habit of tending her sheep, in company with a lad of the same age, whose name was Jean Grenier. The same lad whom Jeanne Gaboriant had questioned.

The little girl often complained to her parents of the conduct of the boy: she said that he frightened her with his horrible stories; but her father and mother thought little of her complaints, till one day she returned home before her usual time so thoroughly alarmed that she had deserted her flock. Her parents now took the matter up and investigated it. Her story was as follows:—

Jean had often told her that he had sold himself to the devil, and that he had acquired the power of ranging the country after dusk, and sometimes in broad day, in the form of a wolf. He had assured her that he had killed and devoured many dogs, but that he found their flesh less palatable than the flesh of little girls, which he regarded as a supreme delicacy. He had told her that this had been tasted by him not unfrequently, but he had specified only two instances: in one he had eaten as much as he could, and had thrown the rest to a wolf, which had come up during the repast. In the other instance he had bitten to death another little girl, had lapped her blood, and, being in a famished condition at the time, had devoured every portion of her, with the exception of the arms and shoulders.

The child told her parents, on the occasion of her return home in a fit of terror, that she had been guiding her sheep as usual, but Grenier had not been present. Hearing a rustle in the bushes she had looked round, and a wild beast had leaped upon her, and torn her clothes on her left side with its sharp fangs. She added that she had defended herself lustily with her shepherd's staff, and had beaten the creature off. It had then retreated a few paces, had seated itself on its hind legs like a dog when it is begging, and had regarded her with such a look of rage, that she had fled in terror. She described the animal as resembling a wolf, but as being shorter and stouter; its hair was red, its tail stumpy, and the head smaller than that of a genuine wolf.

The statement of the child produced general consternation in the parish. It was well known that several little girls had vanished in a most mysterious way of late, and the parents of these little ones were thrown into an agony of terror lest their children had become the prey of the wretched boy accused by Marguerite Poirier. The case was now taken up by the authorities and brought before the parliament of Bordeaux.

The investigation which followed was as complete as could be desired.

Jean Grenier was the son of a poor labourer in the village of S. Antoine de Pizon, and not the son of a priest, as he had asserted. Three months before his seizure he had left home, and had been with several masters doing odd work, or wandering about the country begging. He had been engaged several times to take charge of the flocks belonging to farmers, and had as often been discharged for neglect of his duties. The lad exhibited no reluctance to communicate all he knew about himself, and his statements were tested one by one, and were often proved to be correct.

The story he related of himself before the court was as follows :—

"When I was ten or eleven years old, my neighbour, Duthillaire, introduced me, in the depths of the forest, to a M. de la Forest, a black man, who signed me with his nail, and then gave to me and Duthillaire a salve and a wolf-skin. From that time have I run about the country as a wolf.

"The charge of Marguerite Poirier is correct. My

intention was to have killed and devoured her, but she
kept me off with a stick. I have only killed one dog, a
white one, and I did not drink its blood."

When questioned touching the children, whom he
said he had killed and eaten as a wolf, he allowed that
he had once entered an empty house on the way between
S. Coutras and S. Anlaye, in a small village, the name
of which he did not remember, and had found a child
asleep in its cradle; and as no one was within to hinder
him, he dragged the baby out of its cradle, carried it
into the garden, leaped the hedge, and devoured as
much of it as satisfied his hunger. What remained he
had given to a wolf. In the parish of S. Antoine de
Pizon he had attacked a little girl, as she was keeping
sheep. She was dressed in a black frock; he did not
know her name. He tore her with his nails and teeth,
and ate her. Six weeks before his capture he had fallen
upon another child, near the stone-bridge, in the same
parish. In Eparon he had assaulted the hound of a
certain M. Millon, and would have killed the beast, had
not the owner come out with his rapier in his hand.

Jean said that he had the wolf-skin in his possession, and that he went out hunting for children, at the
command of his master, the Lord of the Forest. Before

transformation he smeared himself with the salve, which he preserved in a small pot, and hid his clothes in the thicket.

He usually ran his courses from one to two hours in the day, when the moon was at the wane, but very often he made his expeditions at night. On one occasion he had accompanied Duthillaire, but they had killed no one.

He accused his father of having assisted him, and of possessing a wolf-skin; he charged him also with having accompanied him on one occasion, when he attacked and ate a girl in the village of Grilland, whom he had found tending a flock of geese. He said that his stepmother was separated from his father. He believed the reason to be, because she had seen him once vomit the paws of a dog and the fingers of a child. He added that the Lord of the Forest had strictly forbidden him to bite the thumb-nail of his left hand, which nail was thicker and longer than the others, and had warned him never to lose sight of it, as long as he was in his were-wolf disguise.

Duthillaire was apprehended, and the father of Jean Grenier himself claimed to be heard by examination.

The account given by the father and stepmother of

Jean coincided in many particulars with the statements made by their son.

The localities where Grenier declared he had fallen on children were identified, the times when he said the deeds had been done accorded with the dates given by the parents of the missing little ones, when their losses had occurred.

The wounds which Jean affirmed that he had made, and the manner in which he had dealt them, coincided with the descriptions given by the children he had assaulted.

He was confronted with Marguerite Poirier, and he singled her out from among five other girls, pointed to the still open gashes in her body, and stated that he had made them with his teeth, when he attacked her in wolf-form, and she had beaten him off with a stick. He described an attack he had made on a little boy whom he would have slain, had not a man come to the rescue, and exclaimed, " I'll have you presently."

The man who saved the child was found, and proved to be the uncle of the rescued lad, and he corroborated the statement of Grenier, that he had used the words mentioned above.

Jean was then confronted with his father. He now

began to falter in his story, and to change his statements. The examination had lasted long, and it was seen that the feeble intellect of the boy was wearied out, so the case was adjourned. When next confronted with the elder Grenier, Jean told his story as at first, without changing it in any important particular.

The fact of Jean Grenier having killed and eaten several children, and of his having attacked and wounded others, with intent to take their life, were fully established; but there was no proof whatever of the father having had the least hand in any of the murders, so that he was dismissed the court without a shadow of guilt upon him.

The only witness who corroborated the assertion of Jean that he changed his shape into that of a wolf was Marguerite Poirier.

Before the court gave judgment, the first president of assize, in an eloquent speech, put on one side all questions of witchcraft and diabolical compact, and bestial transformation, and boldly stated that the court had only to consider the age and the imbecility of the child, who was so dull and idiotic—that children of seven or eight years old have usually a larger amount of reason than he. The president went on to say that Lycan-

thropy and Kuanthropy were mere hallucinations, and
that the change of shape existed only in the disorganized
brain of the insane, consequently it was not a crime
which could be punished. The tender age of the boy
must be taken into consideration, and the utter neglect
of his education and moral development. The court
sentenced Grenier to perpetual imprisonment within the
walls of a monastery at Bordeaux, where he might be
instructed in his Christian and moral obligations; but
any attempt to escape would be punished with death.

A pleasant companion for the monks! a promising
pupil for them to instruct! No sooner was he admitted
into the precincts of the religious house, than he ran
frantically about the cloister and gardens upon all
fours, and finding a heap of bloody and raw offal, fell
upon it and devoured it in an incredibly short space of
time.

Delancre visited him seven years after, and found
him diminutive in stature, very shy, and unwilling to
look any one in the face. His eyes were deep set and
restless; his teeth long and protruding; his nails
black, and in places worn away; his mind was completely barren; he seemed unable to comprehend the
smallest things. He related his story to Delancre, and

told him how he had run about formerly in the woods
as a wolf, and he said that he still felt a craving for raw
flesh, especially for that of little girls, which he said was
delicious, and he added that but for his confinement it
would not be long before he tasted it again. He said
that the Lord of the Forest had visited him twice in the
prison, but that he had driven him off with the sign of
the cross. The account he then gave of his murders
coincided exactly with what had come out in his trial ;
and beside this, his story of the compact he had made
with the Black One, and the manner in which his transformation was effected, also coincided with his former
statements.

He died at the age of twenty, after an imprisonment
of seven years, shortly after Delancre's visit.*

In the two cases of Roulet and Grenier the courts
referred the whole matter of Lycanthropy, or animal
transformation, to its true and legitimate cause, an
aberration of the brain. From this time medical men
seem to have regarded it as a form of mental malady to
be brought under their treatment, rather than as a crime
to be punished by law. But it is very fearful to con-

---

* DELANCRE : *Tableau de l'Inconstance,* p 305.

template that there may still exist persons in the world filled with a morbid craving for human blood, which is ready to impel them to commit the most horrible atrocities, should they escape the vigilance of their guards, or break the bars of the madhouse which restrains them.

CHAPTER VIII.

FOLK-LORE RELATING TO WERE-WOLVES.

Barrenness of English Folk-lore—Devonshire Traditions—Derivation of Were-wolf—Cannibalism in Scotland—The Angus Robber—The Carle of Perth—French Superstitions—Norwegian Traditions—Danish Tales of Were-wolves—Holstein Stories—The Were-wolf in the Netherlands—Among the Greeks; the Serbs; the White Russians; the Poles; the Russians—A Russian Receipt for becoming a Were-wolf—The Bohemian Vilkodlak—Armenian Story—Indian Tales—Abyssinian Budas—American Transformation Tales—A Slovakian Household Tale—Similar Greek, Béarnais, and Icelandic Tales.

ENGLISH folk-lore is singularly barren of were-wolf stories, the reason being that wolves had been extirpated from England under the Anglo-Saxon kings, and therefore ceased to be objects of dread to the people. The traditional belief in were-wolfism must, however, have remained long in the popular mind, though at present it has disappeared, for the word occurs in old ballads and romances. Thus in Kempion—

O was it *war-wolf* in the wood?
    Or was it mermaid in the sea?
Or was it man, or vile woman,
    My ain true love, that mis-shaped thee?

There is also the romance of *William and the Were-wolf* in Hartshorn; [*] but this professes to be a translation from the French :—

> For he of Frenche this fayre tale ferst dede translate,
> In ese of Englysch men in Englysch speche.

In the popular mind the cat or the hare have taken the place of the wolf for witches' transformation, and we hear often of the hags attending the devil's Sabbath in these forms.

In Devonshire they range the moors in the shape of black dogs, and I know a story of two such creatures appearing in an inn and nightly drinking the cider, till the publican shot a silver button over their heads, when they were instantly transformed into two ill-favoured old ladies of his acquaintance. On Heathfield, near Tavistock, the wild huntsman rides by full moon with his "wush hounds;" and a white hare which they pursued was once rescued by a goody returning from market, and discovered to be a transformed young lady.

Gervaise of Tilbury says in his *Otia Imperialia*— "Vidimus frequenter in Anglia, per lunationes, homines in lupos mutari, quod hominum genus *gerulfos* Galli

---

[*] HARTSHORN: *Ancient Metrical Tales*, p. 256. *See* also "The Witch Cake," in CRUMEK's *Remains of Nithsdale Song*.

vocant, Angli vero *wer-wlf*, dicunt: *wer* enim Anglice
virum sonat, *wlf*, lupum." Gervaise may be right in
his derivation of the name, and were-wolf may mean
man-wolf, though I have elsewhere given a different
derivation, and one which I suspect is truer. But
Gervaise has grounds for his assertion that *wér* signifies
man; it is so in Anglo-Saxon, *vair* in Gothic, *vir* in
Latin, *verr*, in Icelandic, *vira*, Zend, *wirs*, old Prussian,
wirs, Lettish, *vira*, Sanskrit, *bîr*, Bengalee.

There have been cases of cannibalism in Scotland,
but no bestial transformation is hinted at in connection
with them.

Thus Bœthius, in his history of Scotland, tells us of
a robber and his daughter who devoured children, and
Lindsay of Pitscottie gives a full account.

" About this time (1460) there was ane brigand ta'en
with his haill family, who haunted a place in Angus.
This mischievous man had ane execrable fashion to take
all young men and children he could steal away quietly,
or tak' away without knowledge, and eat them, and the
younger they were, esteemed them the mair tender
and delicious. For the whilk cause and damnable
abuse, he with his wife and bairns were all
burnt, except ane young wench of a year old who

was saved and brought to Dundee, where she was brought up and fostered; and when she came to a woman's years, she was condemned and burnt quick for that crime. It is said that when she was coming to the place of execution, there gathered ane huge multitude of people, and specially of women, cursing her that she was so unhappy to commit so damnable deeds. To whom she turned about with an ireful countenance, saying :—' Wherefore chide ye with me, as if I had committed ane unworthy act? Give me credence and trow me, if ye had experience of eating men and women's flesh, ye wold think it so delicious that ye wold never forbear it again.' So, but any sign of repentance, this unhappy traitor died in the sight of the people." *

Wyntoun also has a passage in his metrical chronicle regarding a cannibal who lived shortly before his own time, and he may easily have heard about him from surviving contemporaries. It was about the year 1340, when a large portion of Scotland had been devastated by the arms of Edward III.

> About Perth thare was the countrie
> Sae waste, that wonder wes to see;

* LINDSAY's *Chronicles of Scotland*, 1814, p. 163.

> For intill well-great space thereby,
> Wes nother house left nor herb'ry.
> Of deer thare wes then sic foison (profusion),
> That they wold near come to the town,
> Sae great default was near that stead,
> That mony were in hunger dead.
> A carle they said was near thereby,
> That wold set settis (traps) commonly,
> Children and women for to slay,
> And swains that he might over-ta;
> And ate them all that he get might;
> Chwsten Cleek till name behight.
> That sa'ry life continued he,
> While waste but folk was the countrie.*

We have only to compare these two cases with those recorded in the last two chapters, and we see at once how the popular mind in Great Britain had lost the idea of connecting change of form with cannibalism. A man guilty of the crimes committed by the Angus brigand, or the carle of Perth, would have been regarded as a were-wolf in France or Germany, and would have been tried for Lycanthropy.

S. Jerome, by the way, brought a sweeping charge against the Scots. He visited Gaul in his youth, about 380, and he writes:—"When I was a young man in Gaul, I may have seen the Attacotti, a British people who live upon human flesh; and when they find herds

---

* WYNTOUN's *Chronicle*, ii. 236.

of pigs, droves of cattle, or flocks of sheep in the woods, they cut off the haunches of the men and the breasts of the women, and these they regard as great dainties;" in other words they prefer the shepherd to his flock. Gibbon who quotes this passage says on it: "If in the neighbourhood of the commercial and literary town of Glasgow, a race of cannibals has really existed, we may contemplate, in the period of the Scottish history, the opposite extremes of savage and civilized life. Such reflections tend to enlarge the circle of our ideas, and to encourage the pleasing hope that New Zealand may produce in a future age, the Hume of the Southern hemisphere."

If traditions of were-wolves are scanty in England, it is quite the reverse if we cross the water.

In the south of France, it is still believed that fate has destined certain men to be lycanthropists—that they are transformed into wolves at full moon. The desire to run comes upon them at night. They leave their beds, jump out of a window, and plunge into a fountain. After the bath, they come out covered with dense fur, walking on all fours, and commence a raid over fields and meadows, through woods and villages, biting all beasts and human beings that come in their way. At the approach of dawn, they return to the spring, plunge into it, lose their furry skins, and regain their deserted beds. Sometimes the loup-garou is said to appear under the form of a white dog, or to be loaded with chains; but there is probably a confusion of ideas between the were-wolf and the church-dog, bar-ghest, pad-foit, wush-hound, or by whatever name the animal supposed to haunt a churchyard is designated.

In the Périgord, the were-wolf is called louléerou. Certain men, especially bastards, are obliged at each full moon to transform themselves into these diabolic beasts. It is always at night that the fit comes on. The lycanthropist dashes out of a window, springs into a well, and, after having struggled in the water for a few moments, rises from it, dripping, and invested with a goatskin which the devil has given him. In this condition, the louléerous run upon four legs, pass the night in ranging over the country, and in biting and devouring all the dogs they meet. At break of day they lay aside their goatskins and return home. Often they are ill in consequence of having eaten tough old hounds, and they vomit up their undigested paws. One great nuisance to them is the fact that they may be wounded or killed in their louléerou state. With the first effusion of blood their diabolic covering vanishes, and they are recognized, to the disgrace of their families.

A were-wolf may easily be detected, even when devoid of his skin ; for his hands are broad, and his fingers short, and there are always some hairs in the hollow of his hand.

In Normandy, those who are doomed to be loups-garoux, clothe themselves every evening with a skin called their *hère* or *hure*, which is a loan from the devil. When they run in their transformed state, the evil one accompanies them and scourges them at the foot of every cross they pass. The only way in which a were-wolf can be liberated from this cruel bondage, is by stabbing him three times in the forehead with a knife. However, some people less addicted to allopathic treatment, consider that three drops of blood drawn by a needle, will be sufficient to procure release.

According to an opinion of the vulgar in the same province, the loup-garou is sometimes a metamorphosis forced upon the body of a damned person, who, after having been tormented in his grave, has torn his way out of it. The first stage in the process consists in his devouring the cerecloth which enveloped his face ; then his moans and muffled howls ring from the tomb, through the gloom of night, the earth of the grave begins to heave, and at last, with a scream, surrounded by a phosphorescent glare, and exhaling a fœtid odour, he bursts away as a wolf.

In Le Bessin, they attribute to sorcerers the power of metamorphosing certain men into beasts, but the form of a dog is that principally affected by them.

In Norway it is believed that there are persons who can assume the form of a wolf or a bear (Huse-björn), and again resume their own; this property is either imparted to them by the Trollmen, or those possessing it are themselves Trolls.

In a hamlet in the midst of a forest, there dwelt a cottager named Lasse, and his wife. One day he went out in the forest to fell a tree, but had forgot to cross himself and say his paternoster, so that some troll or wolf-witch (varga mor) obtained power over him and transformed him into a wolf. His wife mourned him for many years, but, one Christmas-eve, there came a beggar-woman, very poor and ragged, to the door, and the good woman of the house took her in, fed her well, and entreated her kindly. At her departure the beggar-woman said that the wife would probably see her husband again, as he was not dead, but was wandering in the forest as a wolf. Towards night-fall the wife went to her pantry to place in it a piece of meat for the morrow, when, on turning to go out, she perceived a wolf standing before her, raising itself with its paws on the pantry steps, regarding her with sorrowful and hungry looks. Seeing this she exclaimed, "If I were sure that thou wert my own Lasse, I would give thee a bit of meat." At that instant the wolf-skin fell off, and her husband stood before her in the clothes he wore on the unlucky morning when she had last beheld him.

Finns, Lapps, and Russians are held in particular aversion, because the Swedes believe that they have power to change people into wild beasts. During the last year of the war with Russia, when Calmar was overrun with an unusual number of wolves, it was generally said that the Russians had transformed their Swedish prisoners into wolves, and sent them home to invest the country.

In Denmark the following stories are told:—

A man, who from his childhood had been a were-wolf, when returning one night with his wife from a merry-making, observed that the hour was at hand when the evil usually came upon him; giving therefore the reins to his wife, he descended from the vehicle, saying to her, " If anything comes to thee, only strike at it with thine apron." He then withdrew, but immediately after, the woman, as she was sitting in the vehicle, was attacked by a were-wolf. She did as the man had enjoined her, and struck it with her apron, from which it rived a portion, and then ran away. After some time the man returned, holding in his mouth the rent portion of his wife's apron, on seeing which, she cried out in terror,—" Good Lord, man, why, thou art a were-wolf !" " Thank thee, wife," said he, " now I am free." And from that time he was no more afflicted.

If a female at midnight stretches between four sticks the membrane which envelopes the foal when it is brought forth, and creeps through it, naked, she will bear children without pain ; but all the boys will be were-wolves, and all the girls maras. By day the were-wolf has the human form, though he may be known by the meeting of his eyebrows above the nose. At a certain time of the night he has the form of a dog on three legs. It is only when another person tells him that he is a were-wolf, or reproaches him with being such, that a man can be freed from the ban.

According to a Danish popular song, a hero trans-

formed by his step-mother into a bear, fights with a
knight :—

> For 'tis she who hath bewitched me,
> A woman false and fell,
> Bound an iron girdle round me,
> If thou can'st not break this belt,
> Knight, I'll thee destroy!
> * * * *
> The noble made the Christian sign,
> The girdle snapped, the bear was changed,
> And see! he was a lusty knight,
> His father's realm regained.
>
>   *Kjæmpeviser*, p. 147.

When an old bear in Ofodens Præstegjeld was killed,
after it had caused the death of six men and sixty
horses, it was found to be girded with a similar girdle.

In Schleswig and Holstein they say that if the
were-wolf be thrice addressed by his baptismal name,
he resumes his human form.

On a hot harvest day some reapers lay down in the
field to take their noontide sleep, when one who could
not sleep observed that the fellow next to him rose
softly, and having girded himself with a strap, became a
were-wolf.

A young man belonging to Jägerup returning late
one night from Billund, was attacked, when near
Jägerup, by three were-wolves, and would probably

have been torn to pieces, had he not saved himself by leaping into a rye-field, for there they had no more power over him.

At Caseburg, on the isle of Usedom, a man and his wife were busy in the field making hay, when after some time the woman said to the man that she had no more peace, she could stay no longer, and went away. But she had previously desired her husband to promise, that if perchance a wild beast should come that way, he would cast his hat at it and then run away, and it would do him no injury. She had been gone but a short while, when a wolf came swimming across the Swine, and ran directly towards the haymakers. The man threw his hat at it, which the animal instantly tore to rags. But in the meantime a boy had run up with a pitchfork, and he stabbed the wolf from behind: in the same moment it became changed, and all saw that the boy had killed the man's wife.

Formerly there were individuals in the neighbourhood of Steina, who, by putting on a certain girdle, could transform themselves into were-wolves. A man of the neighbourhood, who had such a girdle, forgot one day when going out to lock it up, as was his wont. During his absence, his little son chanced to find it;

he buckled it round him, and was instantaneously turned into an animal, to all outward appearance like a bundle of peat-straw, and he rolled about like an unwieldy bear. When those who were in the room perceived this, they hastened in search of the father, who was found in time to come and unbuckle the belt, before the child had done any mischief. The boy afterwards said, that when he had put on the girdle, he was seized with such a raging hunger, that he was ready to tear in pieces and devour all that came in his way.

The girdle is supposed to be made of human skin, and to be three finger-breadths wide.

In East Friesland, it is believed, when seven girls succeed each other in one family, that among them one is of necessity a were-wolf, so that youths are slow in seeking one of seven sisters in marriage.

According to a curious Lithuanian story related by Schleicher in his *Litauische Märchen*, a person who is a were-wolf or bear has to remain kneeling in one spot for one hundred years before he can hope to obtain release from his bestial form.

In the Netherlands they relate the following tale :— A man had once gone out with his bow to attend a shooting match at Rousse, but when about half way to the place, he saw on a sudden, a large wolf spring from a thicket, and rush towards a young girl, who was sitting in a meadow by the roadside watching cows. The man did not long hesitate, but quickly drawing forth an arrow, took aim, and luckily hit the wolf in the right side, so that the arrow remained sticking in the wound, and the animal fled howling to the wood.

On the following day he heard that a serving-man of the burgomaster's household lay at the point of death, in consequence of having been shot in the right side, on the preceding day. This so excited the archer's curiosity, that he went to the wounded man, and requested to see the arrow. He recognized it immediately as one of his own. Then, having desired all present to leave the room, he persuaded the man to confess that he was a were-wolf and that he had devoured little children. On the following day he died.

Among the Bulgarians and Slovakians the were-wolf is called *vrkolak*, a name resembling that given it by the modern Greeks βρύκολακας. The Greek were-wolf is closely related to the vampire. The lycanthropist falls into a cataleptic trance, during which his soul leaves his body, enters that of a wolf and ravens for blood. On the return of the soul, the body is exhausted and aches

as though it had been put through violent exercise.
After death lycanthropists become vampires. They are
believed to frequent battlefields in wolf or hyæna shapes,
and to suck the breath from dying soldiers, or to enter
houses and steal the infants from their cradles. Modern
Greeks call any savage-looking man, with dark complexion, and with distorted, misshapen limbs, a
βρύκολακας, and suppose him to be invested with
power of running in wolf-form.

The Serbs connect the vampire and the were-wolf
together, and call them by one name *vlkoslak*. These
rage chiefly in the depths of winter: they hold their
annual gatherings, and at them divest themselves of their
wolf-skins, which they hang on the trees around them.
If any one succeeds in obtaining the skin and burning
it, the vlkoslak is thenceforth disenchanted.

The power to become a were-wolf is obtained by
drinking the water which settles in a foot-print left in
clay by a wolf.

Among the White Russians the *wawkalak* is a man
who has incurred the wrath of the devil, and the evil one
punishes him by transforming him into a wolf and
sending him among his relations, who recognize him
and feed him well. He is a most amiably disposed

were-wolf, for he does no mischief, and testifies his affection for his kindred by licking their hands. He cannot, however, remain long in any place, but is driven from house to house, and from hamlet to hamlet, by an irresistible passion for change of scene. This is an ugly superstition, for it sets a premium on standing well with the evil one.

The Slovakians merrily term a drunkard a vlkodlak, because, forsooth, he makes a beast of himself. A Slovakian household were-wolf tale closes this chapter.

The Poles have their were-wolves, which rage twice in the year—at Christmas and at midsummer.

According to a Polish story, if a witch lays a girdle of human skin on the threshold of a house in which a marriage is being celebrated, the bride and bridegroom, and bridesmaids and groomsmen, should they step across it, are transformed into wolves. After three years, however, the witch will cover them with skins with the hair turned outward; immediately they will recover their natural form. On one occasion, a witch cast a skin of too scanty dimensions over the bridegroom, so that his tail was left uncovered: he resumed his human form, but retained his lupine caudal appendage.

The Russians call the were-wolf *oborot*, which signifies "one transformed." The following receipt is given by them for becoming one.

"He who desires to become an oborot, let him seek in the forest a hewn-down tree; let him stab it with a small copper knife, and walk round the tree, repeating the following incantation :—

On the sea, on the ocean, on the island, on Bujan,
On the empty pasture gleams the moon, on an ashstock lying
In a green wood, in a gloomy vale.
Toward the stock wandereth a shaggy wolf,
Horned cattle seeking for his sharp white fangs;
But the wolf enters not the forest,
But the wolf dives not into the shadowy vale,
Moon, moon, gold-horned moon,
Check the flight of bullets, blunt the hunters' knives,
Break the shepherds' cudgels,
Cast wild fear upon all cattle,
On men, on all creeping things,
That they may not catch the grey wolf,
That they may not rend his warm skin !
My word is binding, more binding than sleep,
More binding than the promise of a hero !

"Then he springs thrice over the tree and runs into the forest, transformed into a wolf."*

In the ancient Bohemian Lexicon of Vacerad (A.D. 1202) the were-wolf is called *vilkodlak*, and is explained as faunus. Safarik says under that head,—

---

* SACHAROW: *Inland*, 1838, No. 17.

"Incubi sepe improbi existunt mulieribus, et earum peragunt concubitum, quos demones Galli *dusios* nuncupant." And in another place: " Vilkodlaci, incubi, sive invidi, ab inviando passim cum animalibus, unde et incubi dicuntur ab incubando homines, i. e. stuprando, quos Romani faunos ficarios dicunt."

That the same belief in lycanthropy exists in Armenia is evident from the following story told by Haxthausen, in his *Trans-Caucasia* (Leipzig, i. 322):—
" A man once saw a wolf, which had carried off a child, dash past him. He pursued it hastily, but was unable to overtake it. At last he came upon the hands and feet of a child, and a little further on he found a cave, in which lay a wolf-skin. This he cast into a fire, and immediately a woman appeared, who howled and tried to rescue the skin from the flames. The man, however, resisted, and, as soon as the hide was consumed, the woman had vanished in the smoke."

In India, on account of the prevalence of the doctrine of metempsychosis, the belief in transformation is widely diffused. Traces of genuine lycanthropy are abundant in all regions whither Buddism has reached. In Ceylon, in Thibet, and in China, we find it still forming a portion of the national creed.

In the Pantschatantra is a story of an enchanted Brahmin's son, who by day was a serpent, by night a man.

Vikramâditya's father, the son of Indra, was condemned to be an ass by day and a man by night.

A modern Indian tale is to this effect:—A prince marries a female ape, but his brothers wed handsome princesses. At a feast given by the queen to her step-daughters, there appears an exquisitely beautiful lady in gorgeous robes. This is none other than the she-ape, who has laid aside her skin for the occasion: the prince slips out of the room and burns the skin, so that his wife is prevented from resuming her favourite appearance.

Nathaniel Pierce * gives an account of an Abyssinian superstition very similar to that prevalent in Europe.

He says that in Abyssinia the gold and silversmiths are highly regarded, but that the ironworkers are looked upon with contempt, as an inferior grade of beings. Their kinsmen even ascribe to them the power of transforming themselves into hyænas, or other savage beasts. All convulsions and hysterical disorders are attributed to the effect of their evil eye. The Amhara

---

* *Life and Adventures of Nathaniel Pierce*, written by himself during a residence in Abyssinia from 1810–19. London, 1831.

call them *Buda*, the Tigré, *Tebbib*. There are also Mahomedan and Jewish Budas. It is difficult to explain the origin of this strange superstition. These Budas are distinguished from other people by wearing gold ear-rings, and Coffin declares that he has often found hyænas with these rings in their ears, even among the beasts which he has shot or speared himself. But how the rings got into their ears is more than Coffin was able to ascertain.

Beside their power to transform themselves into hyænas or other wild beasts, all sorts of other strange things are ascribed to them; and the Abyssinians are firmly persuaded that they rob the graves by midnight, and no one would venture to touch what is called *quanter*, or dried meat in their houses, though they would not object to partake of fresh meat, if they had seen the animal, from which it came, killed before them. Coffin relates, as eye-witness of the fact, the following story :—

Among his servants was a Buda, who, one evening, whilst it was still light, came to his master and asked leave of absence till the following morning. He obtained the required leave and departed; but scarcely had Coffin turned his head, when one of his men exclaimed,—"Look! there he is, changing himself into hyæna," pointing in the direction taken by the Buda. Coffin turned to look, and although he did not witness the process of transformation, the young man had vanished from the spot on which he had been standing, not a hundred paces distant, and in his place was a hyæna running away. The place was a plain without either bush or tree to impede the view. Next morning the young man returned, and was charged by his companions with the transformation: this he rather acknowledged than denied, for he excused himself on the plea that it was the habit of his class. This statement of Pierce is corroborated by a note contributed by Sir Gardner Wilkinson to Rawlinson's *Herodotus* (book iv. chap. 105). "A class of people in Abyssinia are believed to change themselves into hyænas when they like. On my appearing to discredit it, I was told by one who lived for years there, that no well-informed person doubted it, and that he was once walking with one of them, when he happened to look away for a moment, and on turning again towards his companion, he saw him trotting off in the shape of a hyæna. He met him afterwards in his old form. These worthies are blacksmiths.—G. W."

A precisely similar superstition seems to have existed in America, for Joseph Acosta (*Hist. Nat. des Indes*) relates that the ruler of a city in Mexico, who was sent for by the predecessor of Montezuma, transformed himself, before the eyes of those who were sent to seize him, into an eagle, a tiger, and an enormous serpent. He yielded at last, and was condemned to death. No longer in his own house, he was unable to work miracles so as to save his life. The Bishop of Chiapa, a province of Guatemala, in a writing published in 1702, ascribes the same power to the Naguals, or national priests, who laboured to bring back to the religion of their ancestors, the children brought up as Christians by the government. After various ceremonies, when the child instructed advanced to embrace him, the Nagual suddenly assumed a frightful aspect, and under the form of a lion or tiger, appeared chained to the young Christian convert.—(*Recueil de Voyages*, tom. ii. 187.)

Among the North American Indians, the belief in transformation is very prevalent. The following story closely resembles one very prevalent all over the world.

" One Indian fixed his residence on the borders of the Great Bear lake, taking with him only a dog big

with young. In due time, this dog brought forth eight pups. Whenever the Indian went out to fish, he tied up the pups, to prevent the straying of the litter. Several times, as he approached his tent, he heard noises proceeding from it, which sounded like the talking, the laughing, the crying, the wail, and the merriment of children ; but, on entering it, he only perceived the pups tied up as usual. His curiosity being excited by the noises he had heard, he determined to watch and learn whence these sounds proceeded, and what they were. One day he pretended to go out to fish, but, instead of doing so, he concealed himself in a convenient place. In a short time he again heard voices, and, rushing suddenly into the tent, beheld some beautiful children sporting and laughing, with the dog-skins lying by their side. He threw the dog-skins into the fire, and the children, retaining their proper forms, grew up, and were the ancestors of the dog-rib nation."
—(*Traditions of the North American Indians*, by T. A. Jones, 1830, vol. ii. p. 18.)

In the same work is a curious story entitled *The Mother of the World*, which bears a close analogy to another world-wide myth : a woman marries a dog, by night the dog lays aside its skin, and appears as a man.

This may be compared with the tale of Björn and Bera already given.

I shall close this chapter with a Slovakian household tale given by T. T. Hanush in the third volume of *Zeitschrift für Deutsche Mythologie*.

The Daughter of the Vlkolak.

" THERE was once a father, who had nine daughters, and they were all marriageable, but the youngest was the most beautiful. The father was a were-wolf. One day it came into his head : ' What is the good of having to support so many girls?' so he determined to put them all out of the way.

" He went accordingly into the forest to hew wood, and he ordered his daughters to let one of them bring him his dinner. It was the eldest who brought it.

" ' Why, how come you so early with the food?' asked the woodcutter.

" ' Truly, father, I wished to strengthen you, lest you should fall upon us, if famished!'

" ' A good lass!   Sit down whilst I eat.'   He ate, and whilst he ate he thought of a scheme.   He rose and said : ' My girl, come, and I will show you a pit I have been digging.'

"'And what is the pit for?'

"'That we may be buried in it when we die, for poor folk will not be cared for much after they are dead and gone.'

"So the girl went with him to the side of the deep pit. 'Now hear,' said the were-wolf, 'you must die and be cast in there.'

"She begged for her life, but all in vain, so he laid hold of her and cast her into the grave. Then he took a great stone and flung it in upon her and crushed her head, so the poor thing breathed out her soul. When the were-wolf had done this he went back to his work, and as dusk came on, the second daughter arrived, bringing him food. He told her of the pit, and brought her to it, and cast her in, and killed her as the first. And so he dealt with all his girls up to the last. The youngest knew well that her father was a were-wolf, and she was grieved that her sisters did not return; she thought, 'Now where can they be? Has my father kept them for companionship; or to help him in his work?' So she made the food which she was to take him, and crept cautiously through the wood. When she came near the place where her father worked, she heard his strokes felling timber, and smelt smoke. She saw presently a large fire and two human heads roasting at it. Turning from the fire, she went in the direction of the axe-strokes, and found her father.

"'See,' said she, 'father, I have brought you food.'

"'That is a good lass,' said he. 'Now stack the wood for me whilst I eat.'

"'But where are my sisters?' she asked.

"'Down in yon valley drawing wood,' he replied; 'follow me, and I will bring you to them.'

"They came to the pit; then he told her that he had dug it for a grave. 'Now,' said he, 'you must die, and be cast into the pit with your sisters.'

"'Turn aside, father,' she asked, 'whilst I strip off my clothes, and then slay me if you will.'

"He turned aside as she requested, and then— tchich! she gave him a push, and he tumbled headlong into the hole he had dug for her.

"She fled for her life, for the were-wolf was not injured, and he soon would scramble out of the pit.

"Now she hears his howls resounding through the gloomy alleys of the forest, and swift as the wind she runs. She hears the tramp of his approaching feet, and the snuffle of his breath. Then she casts behind her her handkerchief. The were-wolf seizes this with teeth and nails, and rends it till it is reduced to tiny ribands. In another moment he is again in pursuit foaming at the mouth, and howling dismally, whilst his red eyes gleam like burning coals. As he gains on her, she casts behind her her gown, and bids him tear that. He seizes the gown and rives it to shreds, then again he pursues. This time she casts behind her her apron, next her petticoat, then her shift, and at last runs much in the condition in which she was born. Again the were-wolf approaches; she bounds out of the forest into a hay-field, and hides herself in the smallest heap of hay. Her father enters the field, runs howling about it in search of her, cannot find her, and begins to upset the different haycocks, all the while growling and gnashing his gleaming white fangs in his rage at her having escaped him. The foam flakes drop at every step from his mouth, and his skin is reeking with sweat. Before he has reached the smallest bundle of hay his strength leaves him, he feels exhaustion begin to creep over him, and he retires to the forest.

" The king goes out hunting every day; one of his dogs carries food to the hay-field, which has most unaccountably been neglected by the hay-makers for three days. The king, following the dog, discovers the fair - damsel, not exactly 'in the straw,' but up to her neck in hay. She is carried, hay and all, to the palace, where she becomes his wife, making only one stipulation before becoming his bride, and that is, that no beggar shall be permitted to enter the palace.

"After some years a beggar does get in, the beggar being, of course, none other than her were-wolf father. He steals upstairs, enters the nursery, cuts the throats of the two children borne by the queen to her lord, and lays the knife under her pillow.

"In the morning, the king, supposing his wife to be the murderess, drives her from home, with the dead princes hung about her neck. A hermit comes to the rescue, and restores the babies to life. The king finds out his mistake, is reunited to the lady out of the hay, and the were-wolf is cast off a high cliff into the sea, and that is the end of *him*. The king, the queen, and the princes live happily, and may be living yet, for no notice of their death has appeared in the newspaper."

This story bears some resemblance to one told by Von Hahn in his *Griechische und Albanesische Märchen ;* I remember having heard a very similar one in the Pyrenees ; but the man who flies from the were-wolf is one who, after having stripped off all his clothes, rushes into a cottage and jumps into a bed. The were-wolf dares not, or cannot, follow. The cause of his flight was also different. He was a freemason who had divulged the secret, and the were-wolf was the master of his lodge in pursuit of him. In the Bearnais story, there is nothing similar to the last part of the Slovakian tale, and in the Greek one the transformation and the pursuit are omitted, though the woman-eater is called " dog's-head," much as an outlaw in the north of Europe was said to be wolf-headed.

It is worthy of notice in the tale of *The Daughter of the Ulkolak*, that the were-wolf fit is followed by great exhaustion,* and that the wolf is given clothes to tear, much as in the Danish stories already related. There does not seem to be any indication of his having changed his shape, at least no change is mentioned, his hands are spoken of, and he swears and curses his daughter in broad Slovakian. The fit very closely resembles that to which Skallagrim, the Icelander, was subject. It is a pity that the maid Bràk in the Icelandic tale did not fall upon her legs like the young lady in the hay.

---

* Compare this with the exhaustion following a Berserkir fit, and that which succeeded the attacks to which M. Bertrand was subject.

CHAPTER IX.

NATURAL CAUSES OF LYCANTHROPY.

Innate Cruelty—Its Three Forms—Dumollard—Andreas Bichel—A
Dutch Priest—Other instances of Inherent Cruelty—Cruelty united
to Refinement—A Hungarian Bather in Blood—Suddenness with
which the Passion is developed—Cannibalism ; in pregnant Women ;
in Maniacs—Hallucination; How Produced—Salves—The Story of
Lucius—Self-deception.

WHAT I have related from the chronicles of antiquity,
or from the traditional lore of the people, is veiled
under the form of myth or legend; and it is only from
Scandinavian descriptions of those afflicted with the
wolf-madness, and from the trials of those charged with
the crime of lycanthropy in the later Middle Ages, that
we can arrive at the truth respecting that form of madness which was invested by the superstitious with so
much mystery.

It was not till the close of the Middle Ages that

lycanthropy was recognized as a disease; but it is one which has so much that is ghastly and revolting in its form, and it is so remote from all our ordinary experience, that it is not surprising that the casual observer should leave the consideration of it, as a subject isolated and perplexing, and be disposed to regard as a myth that which the feared investigation might prove a reality.

In this chapter I purpose briefly examining the conditions under which men have been regarded as werewolves.

Startling though the assertion may be, it is a matter of fact, that man, naturally, in common with other carnivora, is actuated by an impulse to kill, and by a love of destroying life.

It is positively true that there are many to whom the sight of suffering causes genuine pleasure, and in whom the passion to kill or torture is as strong as any other passion. Witness the number of boys who assemble around a sheep or pig when it is about to be killed, and who watch the struggle of the dying brute with hearts beating fast with pleasure, and eyes sparkling with delight. Often have I seen an eager crowd of children assembled around the slaughterhouses of French towns, absorbed in the expiring agonies of the sheep and cattle, and hushed into silence as they watched the flow of blood.

The propensity, however, exists in different degrees. In some it is manifest simply as indifference to suffering, in others it appears as simple pleasure in seeing killed, and in others again it is dominant as an irresistible desire to torture and destroy.

This propensity is widely diffused; it exists in children and adults, in the gross-minded and the refined, in the well-educated and the ignorant, in those who have never had the opportunity of gratifying it, and those who gratify it habitually, in spite of morality, religion, laws, so that it can only depend on constitutional causes.

The sportsman and the fisherman follow a natural instinct to destroy, when they make war on bird, beast, and fish: the pretence that the spoil is sought for the table cannot be made with justice, as the sportsman cares little for the game he has obtained, when once it is consigned to his pouch. The motive for his eager pursuit of bird or beast must be sought elsewhere; it will be found in the natural craving to extinguish life, which exists in his soul. Why does a child impulsively strike at a butterfly as it flits past him? He cares nothing for the insect when once it is beaten down at his feet, unless it be quivering in its agony, when he will watch it with interest. The child strikes at the fluttering creature because it has *life* in it, and he has an instinct within him impelling him to destroy life wherever he finds it.

Parents and nurses know well that children by nature are cruel, and that humanity has to be acquired by education. A child will gloat over the sufferings of a wounded animal till his mother bids him "put it out of its misery." An unsophisticated child would not dream of terminating the poor creature's agonies abruptly, any more than he would swallow whole a bon-bon till he had well sucked it. Inherent cruelty may be obscured by after impressions, or may be kept under moral restraint; the person who is constitutionally a Nero, may scarcely know his own nature, till by some accident the master passion becomes dominant, and sweeps all before it. A relaxation of the moral check, a shock to the controlling intellect, an abnormal condition of body, are sufficient to allow the passion to assert itself.

As I have already observed, this passion exists in different persons in different degrees.

In some it is exhibited in simple want of feeling for other people's sufferings. This temperament may lead to crime, for the individual who is regardless of pain in another, will be ready to destroy that other, if it suit his own purposes. Such an one was the pauper Dumollard, who was the murderer of at least six poor girls, and who attempted to kill several others. He seems not to have felt much gratification in murdering them, but to have been so utterly indifferent to their sufferings, that he killed them solely for the sake of their clothes, which were of the poorest description. He was sentenced to the guillotine, and executed in 1862.*

In others, the passion for blood is developed alongside with indifference to suffering.

Thus Andreas Bichel enticed young women into his house, under the pretence that he was possessed of a magic mirror, in which he would show them their future husbands; when he had them in his power he bound their hands behind their backs, and stunned them with a blow. He then stabbed them and despoiled them of their clothes, for the sake of which he committed the murders; but as he killed the young women

---

* A full account of this man's trial is given by one who was present, in *All the Year Round*, No. 162.

the passion of cruelty took possession of him, and he hacked the poor girls to pieces whilst they were still alive, in his anxiety to examine their insides. Catherine Seidel he opened with a hammer and a wedge, from her breast downwards, whilst still breathing. "I may say," he remarked at his trial, "that during the operation I was so eager, that I trembled all over, and I longed to rive off a piece and eat it."

Andreas Bichel was executed in 1809.[*]

Again, a third class of persons are cruel and bloodthirsty, because in them bloodthirstiness is a raging insatiable passion. In a civilized country those possessed by this passion are forced to control it through fear of the consequences, or to gratify it upon the brute creation. But in earlier days, when feudal lords were supreme in their domains, there have been frightful instances of their excesses, and the extent to which some of the Roman emperors indulged their passion for blood is matter of history.

Gall gives several authentic instances of bloodthirstiness.[†]   A Dutch priest had such a desire to kill

---

[*] The case of Andreas Bichel is given in Lady Duff Gordon's *Remarkable Criminal Trials.*

[†] GALL: *Sur les Fonctions du Cerveau*, tom. iv.

and to see killed, that he became chaplain to a regiment that he might have the satisfaction of seeing deaths occurring wholesale in engagements. The same man kept a large collection of various kinds of domestic animals, that he might be able to torture their young. He killed the animals for his kitchen, and was acquainted with all the hangmen in the country, who sent him notice of executions, and he would walk for days that he might have the gratification of seeing a man executed.

In the field of battle the passion is variously developed; some feel positive delight in slaying, others are indifferent. An old soldier, who had been in Waterloo, informed me that to his mind there was no pleasure equal to running a man through the body, and that he could lie awake at night musing on the pleasurable sensations afforded him by that act.

Highwaymen are frequently not content with robbery, but manifest a bloody inclination to torment and kill. John Rosbeck, for instance, is well known to have invented and exercised the most atrocious cruelties, merely that he might witness the sufferings of his victims, who were especially women and children. Neither fear nor torture could break him of the dreadful passion till he was executed.

Gall tells of a violin-player, who, being arrested, confessed to thirty-four murders, all of which he had committed, not from enmity or intent to rob, but solely because it afforded him an intense pleasure to kill.

Spurzheim * tells of a priest at Strasbourg, who, though rich, and uninfluenced by envy or revenge, from exactly the same motive, killed three persons.

Gall relates the case of a brother of the Duke of Bourbon, Condé, Count of Charlois, who, from infancy, had an inveterate pleasure in torturing animals : growing older, he lived to shed the blood of human beings, and to exercise various kinds of cruelty. He also murdered many from no other motive, and shot at slaters for the pleasure of seeing them fall from the roofs of houses.

Louis XI. of France caused the death of 4,000 people during his reign ; he used to watch their executions from a neighbouring lattice. He had gibbets placed outside his own palace, and himself conducted the executions.

It must not be supposed that cruelty exists merely in the coarse and rude ; it is quite as frequently observed in the refined and educated. Among the former it is

---

* *Doctrine of the Mind,* p. 158.

manifest chiefly in insensibility to the sufferings of others; in the latter it appears as a passion, the indulgence of which causes intense pleasure.

Those bloody tyrants, Nero and Caligula, Alexander Borgia, and Robespierre, whose highest enjoyment consisted in witnessing the agonies of their fellow-men, were full of delicate sensibilities and great refinement of taste and manner.

I have seen an accomplished young woman of considerable refinement and of a highly strung nervous temperament, string flies with her needle on a piece of thread, and watch complacently their flutterings. Cruelty may remain latent till, by some accident. it is aroused, and then it will break forth in a devouring flame. It is the same with the passion for blood as with the passions of love and hate; we have no conception of the violence with which they can rage till circumstances occur which call them into action. Love or hate will be dominant in a breast which has been in serenity, till suddenly the spark falls, passion blazes forth, and the serenity of the quiet breast is shattered for ever. A word, a glance, a touch, are sufficient to fire the magazine of passion in the heart, and to desolate for ever an existence. It is the same with bloodthirstiness. It may lurk in the deeps of some heart very dear to us. It may smoulder in the bosom which is most cherished by us, and we may be perfectly unconscious of its existence there. Perhaps circumstances will not cause its development; perhaps moral principle may have bound it down with fetters it can never break.

Michael Wagener* relates a horrible story which occurred in Hungary, suppressing the name of the person, as it was that of a still powerful family in the country. It illustrates what I have been saying, and shows how trifling a matter may develope the passion in its most hideous proportions.

" Elizabeth —— was wont to dress well in order to please her husband, and she spent half the day over her toilet. On one occasion, a lady's-maid saw something wrong in her head-dress, and as a recompence for observing it, received such a severe box on the ears that the blood gushed from her nose, and spirted on to her mistress's face. When the blood drops were washed off her face, her skin appeared much more beautiful—whiter and more transparent on the spots where the blood had been.

" Elizabeth formed the resolution to bathe her face

---

* *Beitrage zur philosophischen Anthropologie*, Wien, 1796.

and her whole body in human blood so as to enhance her beauty. Two old women and a certain Fitzko assisted her in her undertaking. This monster used to kill the luckless victim, and the old women caught the blood, in which Elizabeth was wont to bathe at the hour of four in the morning. After the bath she appeared more beautiful than before.

" She continued this habit after the death of her husband (1604) in the hopes of gaining new suitors. The unhappy girls who were allured to the castle, under the plea that they were to be taken into service there, were locked up in a cellar. Here they were beaten till their bodies were swollen. Elizabeth not unfrequently tortured the victims herself; often she changed their clothes which dripped with blood, and then renewed her cruelties. The swollen bodies were then cut up with razors.

" Occasionally she had the girls burned, and then cut up, but the great majority were beaten to death.

" At last her cruelty became so great, that she would stick needles into those who sat with her in a carriage, especially if they were of her own sex. One of her servant-girls she stripped naked, smeared her with honey, and so drove her out of the house.

" When she was ill, and could not indulge her cruelty, she bit a person who came near her sick bed as though she were a wild beast.

" She caused, in all, the death of 650 girls, some in Tscheita, on the neutral ground, where she had a cellar constructed for the purpose ; others in different localities; for murder and bloodshed became with her a necessity.

" When at last the parents of the lost children could no longer be cajoled, the castle was seized, and the traces of the murders were discovered.   Her accomplices were executed, and she was imprisoned for life."

An equally remarkable example will be found in the account of the Mareschal de Retz given at some length in the sequel. He was an accomplished man, a scholar, an able general, and a courtier ; but suddenly the impulse to murder and destroy came upon him whilst sitting in the library reading *Suetonius ;* he yielded to the impulse, and became one of the greatest monsters of cruelty the world has produced.

The case of Sviatek, the Gallician cannibal, is also to the purpose. This man was a harmless pauper, till one day accident brought him to the scene of a confla- gration. Hunger impelled him to taste of the roast fragments of a human being who had perished in the fire, and from that moment he ravened for man's flesh.

M. Bertrand was a French gentleman of taste and education. He one day lounged over the churchyard wall in a quiet country village and watched a funeral. Instantly an overwhelming desire to dig up and rend the corpse which he had seen committed to the ground came upon him, and for years he lived as a human hyæna, preying upon the dead. His story is given in detail in the fifteenth chapter.

An abnormal condition of body sometimes produces this desire for blood. It is manifest in certain cases of pregnancy, when the constitution loses its balance, and the appetite becomes diseased. Schenk* gives instances.

A pregnant woman saw a baker carrying loaves on his bare shoulder. She was at once filled with such a craving for his flesh that she refused to taste any food till her husband persuaded the baker, by the offer of a large sum, to allow his wife to bite him. The man yielded, and the woman fleshed her teeth in his shoulder twice; but he held out no longer. The wife

---

* *Observationes Medic.* lib. iv. De Gravidis.

bore twins on three occasions, twice living, the third time dead.

A woman in an interesting condition, near Andernach on the Rhine, murdered her husband, to whom she was warmly attached, ate half his body, and salted the rest. When the passion left her she became conscious of the horrible nature of her act, and she gave herself up to justice.

In 1553, a wife cut her husband's throat, and gnawed the nose and the left arm, whilst the body was yet warm. She then gutted the corpse, and salted it for future consumption. Shortly after, she gave birth to three children, and she only became conscious of what she had done when her neighbours asked after the father, that they might announce to him the arrival of the little ones.

In the summer of 1845, the Greek papers contained an account of a pregnant woman murdering her husband for the purpose of roasting and eating his liver.

That the passion to destroy is prevalent in certain maniacs is well known; this is sometimes accompanied by cannibalism.

Gruner * gives an account of a shepherd who was

---

* *De Anthropophago Bucano.*   Jen. 1792.

evidently deranged, who killed and ate two men. Marc *
relates that a woman of Unterelsas, during the absence
of her husband, a poor labourer, murdered her son, a lad
fifteen months old. She chopped off his legs and stewed
them with cabbage. She ate a portion, and offered the
rest to her husband. It is true that the family were very
poor, but there was food in the house at the time. In
prison the woman gave evident signs of derangement.

The cases in which bloodthirstiness and cannibalism
are united with insanity are those which properly fall
under the head of Lycanthropy. The instances recorded
in the preceding chapter point unmistakably to hallucination accompanying the lust for blood. Jean Grenier,
Roulet, and others, were firmly convinced that they had
undergone transformation. A disordered condition of
mind or body may produce hallucination in a form
depending on the character and instincts of the individual. Thus, an ambitious man labouring under
monomania will imagine himself to be a king; a
covetous man will be plunged in despair, believing
himself to be penniless, or exult at the vastness of
the treasure which he imagines that he has discovered.

---

* *Die Geistes Krankheiten.*   Berlin, 1844.

The old man suffering from rheumatism or gout conceives himself to be formed of china or glass, and the foxhunter tallyhos! at each new moon, as though he were following a pack. In like manner, the naturally cruel man, if the least affected in his brain, will suppose himself to be transformed into the most cruel and bloodthirsty animal with which he is acquainted.

The hallucinations under which lycanthropists suffered may have arisen from various causes. The older writers, as Forestus and Burton, regard the were-wolf mania as a species of melancholy madness, and some do not deem it necessary for the patient to believe in his transformation for them to regard him as a lycanthropist.

In the present state of medical knowledge, we know that very different conditions may give rise to hallucinations.

In fever cases the sensibility is so disturbed that the patient is often deceived as to the space occupied by his limbs, and he supposes them to be preternaturally distended or contracted. In the case of typhus, it is not uncommon for the sick person, with deranged nervous system, to believe himself to be double in the bed, or to be severed in half, or to have lost his limbs.

He may regard his members as composed of foreign and often fragile materials, as glass, or he may so lose his personality as to suppose himself to have become a woman.

A monomaniac who believes himself to be some one else, seeks to enter into the feelings, thoughts, and habits of the assumed personality, and from the facility with which this is effected, he draws an argument, conclusive to himself, of the reality of the change. He thenceforth speaks of himself under the assumed character, and experiences all its needs, wishes, passions, and the like. The closer the identification becomes, the more confirmed is the monomaniac in his madness, the character of which varies with the temperament of the individual. If the person's mind be weak, or rude and uncultivated, the tenacity with which he clings to his metamorphosis is feebler, and it becomes more difficult to draw the line between his lucid and insane utterances. Thus Jean Grenier, who laboured under this form of mania, said in his trial much that was true, but it was mixed with the ramblings of insanity.

Hallucination may also be produced by artificial means, and there are evidences afforded by the confessions of those tried for lycanthropy, that these artificial means were employed by them.   I refer to the salve so frequently mentioned in witch and were-wolf trials.   The following passage is from the charming *Golden Ass* of Apuleius ; it proves that salves were extensively used by witches for the purpose of transformation, even in his day :—

"Fotis showed me a crack in the door, and bade me look through it, upon which I looked and saw Pamphile first divest herself of all her garments, and then, having unlocked a chest, take from it several little boxes, and open one of the latter, which contained a certain ointment.   Rubbing this ointment a good while previously between the palms of her hands, she anointed her whole body, from the very nails of her toes to the hair on the crown of her head, and when she was anointed all over, she whispered many magic words to a lamp, as if she were talking to it.   Then she began to move her arms, first with tremulous jerks, and afterwards by a gentle undulating motion, till a glittering, downy surface by degrees overspread her body, feathers and strong quills burst forth suddenly, her nose became a hard crooked beak, her toes changed to curved talons, and Pamphile was no longer Pamphile, but it was an owl I saw before me.   And now, uttering a harsh, querulous scream, leaping from the ground by little and little, in order to try her powers, and presently poising herself aloft on her pinions, she stretched forth her wings on either side to their full extent, and flew straight away.

"Having now been actually a witness of the perform-ance of the magical art, and of the metamorphosis of Pamphile, I remained for some time in a stupefied state of astonishment. . . . At last, after I had rubbed my eyes some time, had recovered a little from the amaze-ment and abstraction of mind, and begun to feel a consciousness of the reality of things about me, I took hold of the hand of Fotis and said,—'Sweet damsel, bring me, I beseech thee, a portion of the ointment with which thy mistress hath just now anointed, and when thou hast made me a bird, I will be thy slave, and even wait upon thee like a winged Cupid.' Accordingly she crept gently into the apartment, quickly returned with the box of ointment, hastily placed it in my hands, and then immediately departed.

"Elated to an extraordinary degree at the sight of the precious treasure, I kissed the box several times successively; and uttering repeated aspirations in hopes of a prosperous flight, I stripped off my clothes as quick as possible, dipped my fingers greedily into the box,

and having thence extracted a good large lump of ointment, rubbed it all over my body and limbs. When
I was thoroughly anointed, I swung my arms up and
down, in imitation of the movement of a bird's pinions,
and continued to do so a little while, when instead of
any perceptible token of feathers or wings making their
appearance, my own thin skin, alas! grew into a hard
leathern hide, covered with bristly hair, my fingers and
toes disappeared, the palms of my hands and the soles of
my feet became four solid hoofs, and from the end of my
spine a long tail projected. My face was enormous, my
mouth wide, my nostrils gaping, my lips pendulous,
and I had a pair of immoderately long, rough, hairy
ears. In short, when I came to contemplate my
transformation to its full extent, I found that, instead
of a bird, I had become—an ASS." *

Of what these magical salves were composed we
know. They were composed of narcotics, to wit, *Solanum
somniferum*, aconite, hyoscyamus, belladonna, opium,
acorus vulgaris, sium. These were boiled down with
oil, or the fat of little children who were murdered
for the purpose. The blood of a bat was added, but its

---

* APULEIUS, Sir George Head's translation, bk. iii.

effects could have been *nil*. To these may have been
added other foreign narcotics, the names of which have
not transpired.

Whatever may have been the cause of the hallucination, it is not surprising that the lycanthropist should
have imagined himself transformed into a beast. The
cases I have instanced are those of shepherds, who were
by nature of their employment, brought into collision
with wolves; and it is not surprising that these persons,
in a condition liable to hallucinations, should imagine
themselves to be transformed into wild beasts, and that
their minds reverting to the injuries sustained from these
animals, they should, in their state of temporary insanity,
accuse themselves of the acts of rapacity committed by
the beasts into which they believed themselves to be transformed. It is a well-known fact that men, whose minds
are unhinged, will deliver themselves up to justice,
accusing themselves of having committed crimes which
have actually taken place, and it is only on investigation that their self-accusation proves to be false;
and yet they will describe the circumstances with
the greatest minuteness, and be thoroughly convinced
of their own criminality. I need give but a single
instance.

In the war of the French Revolution, the *Hermione* frigate was commanded by Capt. Pigot, a harsh man and a severe commander. His crew mutinied, and carried the ship into an enemy's port, having murdered the captain and several of the officers, under circumstances of extreme barbarity. One midshipman escaped, by whom many of the criminals, who were afterwards taken and delivered over to justice, one by one, were identified. Mr. Finlayson, the Government actuary, who at that time held an official situation in the Admiralty, states:—"In my own experience I have known, on separate occasions, *more than six sailors* who voluntarily confessed to having struck the first blow at Capt. Pigot. These men detailed all the horrid circumstances of the mutiny with extreme minuteness and perfect accuracy; nevertheless, not one of them had ever been in the ship, nor had so much as seen Capt. Pigot in their lives. They had obtained by tradition, from their messmates, the particulars of the story. When long on a foreign station, hungering and thirsting for home, their minds became enfeebled; at length they actually believed themselves guilty of the crime over which they had so long brooded, and submitted with a gloomy pleasure to being sent to England in irons, for judgment.

At the Admiralty we were always able to detect and
establish their innocence, in defiance of their own
solemn asseverations." — (*London Judicial Gazette*,
January, 1808.)

CHAPTER X.

MYTHOLOGICAL ORIGIN OF THE WERE-WOLF MYTH.

Metempsychosis—Sympathy between Men and Beasts—Finnbog and the Bear—Osage and the Beaver—The connexion of Soul and Body—Buddism—Case of Mr. Holloway—Popular ideas concerning the Body—The derivation of the German Leichnam—Feather Dresses—Transmigration of Souls—A Basque Story—Story from the Pantschatantra—Savage ideas regarding Natural Phenomena—Thunder, Lightning, and Cloud—The origin of the Dragon—John of Bromton's Dragon a Waterspout—The Legend of Typhœus—Allegorizing of the Effects of a Hurricane—Anthropomorphosis—The Cirrus Cloud, a Heavenly Swan—Urvaçi—The Storm-cloud a Dæmon—Vritra and Râkschasas—Story of a Brahmin and a Râkschasas.

TRANSFORMATION into beasts forms an integral portion of all mythological systems. The gods of Greece were wont to change themselves into animals in order to carry out their designs with greater speed, security, and secrecy, than in human forms. In Scandinavian mythology, Odin changed himself into the shape of an eagle, Loki into that of a salmon. Eastern religions abound in stories of transformation.

The line of demarcation between this and the

translation of a beast's soul into man, or a man's soul into a beast's (metempsychosis) is very narrow.

The doctrine of metempsychosis is founded on the consciousness of gradation between beasts and men. The belief in a soul-endowed animal world was present among the ancients, and the laws of intelligence and instinct were misconstrued, or were regarded as a puzzle, which no man might solve.

The human soul with its consciousness seemed to be something already perfected in a pre-existing state, and, in the myth of metempsychosis, we trace the yearnings and gropings of the soul after the source whence its own consciousness was derived, counting its dreams and hallucinations as gleams of memory, recording acts which had taken place in a former state of existence.

Modern philosophy has resumed the same thread of conjecture, and thinks to see in man the perfected development of lower organisms.

After death the translation of the soul was supposed to continue. It became either absorbed into the *nous,* into Brahma, into the deity, or it sank in the scale of creation, and was degraded to animate a brute. Thus the doctrine of metempsychosis was emphatically one of rewards and punishments, for the condition of the soul after death depended on its training during life. A savage and bloodthirsty man was exiled, as in the case of Lycaon, into the body of a wild beast: the soul of a timorous man entered a hare, and drunkards or gluttons became swine.

The intelligence which was manifest in the beasts bore such a close resemblance to that of man, in the childhood and youth of the world, that it is not to be wondered at, if our forefathers failed to detect the line of demarcation drawn between instinct and reason. And failing to distinguish this, they naturally fell into the belief in metempsychosis.

It was not merely a fancied external resemblance between the beast and man, but it was the perception of skill, pursuits, desires, sufferings, and griefs like his own, in the animal creation, which led man to detect within the beast something analogous to the soul within himself; and this, notwithstanding the points of contrast existing between them, elicited in his mind so strong a sympathy that, without a great stretch of imagination, he invested the beast with his own attributes, and with the full powers of his own understanding. He regarded it as actuated by the same motives, as subject to the same laws of honour, as moved by the same prejudices, and the higher the beast was in the scale, the more he regarded it as an equal.   A singular illustration of this will be found in the Finnboga Saga, c. xi.

"Now we must relate about Finnbog.   Afterward in the evening, when men slept, he rose, took his weapons, and went forth, following the tracks which led to the dairy farm.   As was his wont, he stepped out briskly along the spoor till he came to the dairy.   There he found the bear lying down, and he had slain the sheep, and he was lying on them lapping their blood.   Then said Finnbog : ' Stand up, Bruin! make ready against me ; that becomes you more than crouching over those sheep's carcases.'

" The bear sat up, looked at him, and lay down again.   Finnbog said, ' If you think that I am too fully armed to match with you, I will do this,' and he took off his helmet and laid aside his shield.   Then he said, ' Stand up now, if you dare ! '

" The bear sat up, shook his head, and then cast himself down again.   " Finnbog exclaimed, ' I see, you want us both to be *boune* alike ! ' so he flung aside his sword and said, ' Be it as you will; now stand up if you have the heart that I believe you have, rather than one such as was possessed by these rent sheep.'

"Then Bruin stood up and prepared to fight."

The following story taken from the mouth of an Osage Indian by J. A. Jones, and published in his *Traditions of the North American Indians,* shows how thoroughly the savage mind misses the line of demarcation between instinct and reason, and how the man of the woods looks upon beasts as standing on an equality with himself.

An Osage warrior is in search of a wife: he admires the tidy and shrewd habits of the beaver. He accordingly goes to a beaver-hut to obtain one of that race for a bride. "In one corner of the room sat a beaver-woman combing the heads of some little beavers, whose ears she boxed very soundly when they would not lie still. The warrior, *i. e.* the beaver-chief, whispered the Osage that she was his second wife, and was very apt to be cross when there was work to be done, which prevented her from going to see her neighbours. Those whose heads she was combing were her children, he said, and she who had made them rub their noses against each other and be friends, was his eldest daughter. Then calling aloud, 'Wife,' said he, 'what have you to eat? The stranger is undoubtedly hungry; see, he is pale, his eye has no fire, and his step is like that of a moose.'

"Without replying to him, for it was a sulky day with her, she called aloud, and a dirty-looking beaver entered. 'Go,' said she, 'and fetch the stranger something to eat.' With that the beaver girl passed through a small door into another room, from which she soon returned, bringing some large pieces of willow-bark, which she laid at the feet of the warrior and his guest. While the warrior-beaver was chewing the willow, and the Osage was pretending to do so, they fell to talking over many matters, particularly the wars of the beavers with the otters, and their frequent victories over them. He told our father by what means the beavers felled large trees, and moved them to the places where they wished to make dams; how they raised to an erect position the poles for their lodges, and how they plastered them so as to keep out rain. Then he spoke of their employments when they had buried the hatchet; of the peace and happiness and tranquillity they en-joyed when gathered into companies, they rested from their labours, and passed their time in talking and feasting, and bathing, and playing the game of bones, and making love. All the while the young beaver-maiden sat with her eyes fixed upon the Osage, at every pause moving a little nearer, till at length she was at

his side with her forepaw upon his arm; a minute more
and she had placed it around his neck, and was rubbing
her soft furry cheek against his.   Our ancestor, on his
part, betrayed no disinclination to receive her caresses,
but returned them with equal ardour.   The old beaver
seeing what was going on, turned his back upon them,
and suffered them to be as kind to each other as they
pleased.   At last, turning quickly round, while the
maiden, suspecting what was coming, and pretending to
be abashed, ran behind her mother, he said, ' To end
this foolery, what say you to marrying my daughter?
She is well brought up, and is the most industrious girl
in the village.   She will flap more wall with her tail
in a day than any maiden in the nation; she will gnaw
down a larger tree betwixt the rising of the sun and the
coming of the shadows than many a smart beaver of the
other sex.   As for her wit, try her at the game of the
dish, and see who gets up master; and for cleanliness,
look at her petticoat?'   Our father answered that he
did not doubt that she was industrious and cleanly,
able to gnaw down a very large tree, and to use her tail
to very good' purpose; that he loved her much, and
wished to make her the mother of his children.   And
thereupon the bargain was concluded."

These two stories, the one taken from Icelandic saga, the other from American Indian tradition, shew clearly the oneness which the uncultivated mind believes to exist between the soul of man and the soul of beast. The same sentiments actuate both man and brute, and if their actions are unlike, it is because of the difference in their formation. The soul within is identical, but the external accidents of body are unlike.

Among many rude as well as cultivated people, the body is regarded as a mere garment wrapped around the soul. The Buddist looks upon identity as existing in the soul alone, and the body as no more constituting identity, than the clothes he puts on or takes off. He exists as a spirit; for convenience he vests himself in a body; sometimes that body is human, sometimes it is bestial. As his soul rises in the spiritual scale, the nobler is the animal form which it tenants. Budda himself passed through various stages of existence; in one he was a hare, and his soul being noble, led him to immolate himself, in order that he might offer hospitality to Indra, who, in the form of an old man, craved of him food and shelter. The Buddist regards animals with reverence; an ancestor may be tenanting the body of the ox he is driving, or a descendant may be running at his side barking and wagging his tail. When he falls into an ecstasy, his soul is leaving his body for a little while, it is laying aside its raiment of flesh and blood and bone, to return to it once more when the trance is over. But this idea is not confined to Buddists, it is common everywhere. The spirit or soul is supposed to be imprisoned in the body, the body is but the lantern through which the spirit shines, " the corruptible body" is believed to "press down the soul," and the soul is unable to attain to perfect happiness till it has shuffled off this earthy coil. Butler regards the members of the body as so many instruments used by the soul for the purpose of seeing, hearing, feeling, &c., just as we use telescopes or crutches, and which may be rejected without injury to our individuality.

The late Mr. J. Holloway, of the Bank of England, brother to the engraver of that name, related of himself that, being one night in bed, and unable to sleep, he had fixed his eyes and thoughts with uncommon intensity on a beautiful star that was shining in at the window, when he suddenly found his spirit released from his body and soaring into space. But instantly seized with anxiety for the anguish of his wife, if she discovered his body apparently dead beside her, he returned, and re-entered it with difficulty. He described that returning as a returning from light into *darkness*, and that whilst the spirit was free, he was alternately in the light or the dark, accordingly as his thoughts were with his wife or with the star. Popular mythology in most lands regards the soul as oppressed by the body, and its liberation is considered a deliverance from the "burden" of the flesh. Whether the soul is at all able to act or express itself without a body, any more than a fire is able to make cloth without the apparatus of boiler and machinery, is a question which has not commended itself to the popular mind. But it may be remarked that the Christian religion alone is that which raises the body to a dignity equal to that of the soul, and gives it a hope of ennoblement and resurrection never dreamed of in any mythological system.

But the popular creed, in spite of the most emphatic testimony of Scripture, is that the soul is in bondage so long as it is united to a body, a creed entirely in accordance with that of Buddism.

If the body be but the cage, as a poet * of our own has been pleased to call it, in which dwells the imprisoned soul, it is quite possible for the soul to change

---

* VAUGHAN, *Silex Scintillans.*

its cage. If the body be but a vesture clothing the soul, as the Buddist asserts, it is not improbable that it may occasionally change its vesture.

This is self-evident, and thus have arisen the countless tales of transformation and transmigration which are found all over the world. That the same view of the body as a mere clothing of the soul was taken by our Teutonic and Scandinavian ancestors, is evident even from the etymology of the words *leichnam, likhama,* used to express the soulless body.

I have already spoken of the Norse word *hamr,* I wish now to make some further remarks upon it. *Hamr* is represented in Anglo-Saxon by *hama, homa,* in Saxon by *hamo,* in old High German by *hamo,* in old French by *homa, hama,* to which are related the Gothic *gahamon, ufar-hamon, ana-hamon,* ἐνδύεσθαι, ἐπενδύεσθαι; *and-hamon, af-hamon,* ἀπεκδύειν, ἐκδύεσθαι· thence also the old High German *hemidi,* and the modern *Hemde,* garment. In composition we find this word, as *lik-hamr,* in old Norse; in old High German *lik-hamo,* Anglo-Saxon *lik-hama,* and *flœsc-hama,* Old Saxon, *lik-hamo,* modern German *Leich-nam,* a body, *i. e.* a garment of flesh, precisely as the bodies of birds are called in old Norse *fjaðr-hamr,* in Anglo-Saxon

feðerhoma, in Old Saxon fetherhamo, or feather-dresses ;
and the bodies of wolves are called in old Norse
úlfshamr, and seals' bodies in Faroëse kópahamr. The
significance of the old verb að hamaz is now evident ;
it is to migrate from one body to another, and hama-
skipti is a transmigration of the soul. The method of
this transmigration consisted in simply investing the
body with the skin of the animal into which the soul
was to migrate. When Loki, the Northern god of evil,
went in quest of the stolen Idunn, he borrowed of
Freyja her falcon dress, and at once became, to all
intents and purposes, a falcon. Thiassi pursued him
as he left Thrymheimr, having first taken upon him an
eagle's dress, and thereby become an eagle.

In order to seek Thor's lost hammer, Loki borrowed again of Freyja her feather dress, and as he flew
away in it, the feathers sounded as they winnowed the
breeze (fjaðrhamr dunði).

In like manner Cædmon speaks of an evil spirit
flying away in feather-dress : "þät he mid feðerhomon
fleôgan meahte, windan on wolkne" (Gen. ed. Gr. 417),
and of an angel, " þuo þar suogan quam engil þes
alowaldon obhana fun radure faran an feðerhamon "
(Hêlj. 171, 23), the very expression made use of when

speaking of a bird: "farad an feĉarhamun" (Hêlj. 50, 11).

The soul, in certain cases, is able to free itself from the body and to enter that of beast or man— in this form stood the myth in various theological systems.

Among the Finns and Lapps it is not uncommon for a magician to fall into a cataleptic condition, and during the period his soul is believed to travel very frequently in bodily form, having assumed that of any animal most suitable for its purpose. I have given instances in a former chapter. The same doctrine is evident in most cases of lycanthropy. The patient is in a state of trance, his body is watched, and it remains motionless, but his soul has migrated into the carcase of a wolf, which it vivifies, and in which it runs its course. A curious Basque story shows that among this strange Turanian people, cut off by such a flood of Aryan nations from any other members of its family, the same superstition remains. A huntsman was once engaged in the chase of a bear among the Pyreneean peaks, when Bruin turned suddenly on him and hugged him to death, but not before he had dealt the brute its mortal wound. As the huntsman expired, he breathed his soul into the body of the bear, and thenceforward ranged the mountains as a beast.

One of the tales of the Sanskrit book of fables, the *Pantschatantra,* affords such a remarkable testimony to the Indian belief in metempsychosis, that I am tempted to give it in abstract.

A king was one day passing through the market-place of his city, when he observed a hunchbacked merryandrew, whose contortions and jokes kept the bystanders in a roar of laughter. Amused with the fellow, the king brought him to his palace. Shortly after, in the hearing of the clown, a necromancer taught the monarch the art of sending his soul into a body not his own.

Some little while after this, the monarch, anxious to put in practice his newly acquired knowledge, rode into the forest accompanied by his fool, who, he believed, had not heard, or, at all events comprehended, the lesson. They came upon the corpse of a Brahmin lying in the depth of the jungle, where he had died of thirst. The king, leaving his horse, performed the requisite ceremony, and instantly his soul had migrated into the body of the Brahmin, and his own lay as dead upon the ground. At the same moment,

however, the hunchback deserted his body, and possessed
himself of that which had been the king's, and shouting
farewell to the dismayed monarch, he rode back to the
palace, where he was received with royal honours.   But
it was not long before the queen and one of the ministers
discovered that a screw was somewhere loose, and when
the quondam king, but now Brahmin, arrived and told
his tale, a plot was laid for the recovery of his body.
The queen asked her false husband whether it were
possible to make her parrot talk, and he in a moment
of uxorious weakness promised to make it speak.   He
laid his body aside, and sent his soul into the parrot.
Immediately the true king jumped out of his Brahmin
body and resumed that which was legitimately his own,
and then proceeded, with the queen, to wring the neck
of the parrot.

But besides the doctrine of metempsychosis, which
proved such a fertile mother of fable, there was another
article of popular mythology which gave rise to stories
of transformation.   Among the abundant superstitions
existing relative to transformation, three shapes seem to
have been pre-eminently affected—that of the swan, that
of the wolf, and that of the serpent.   In many of the
stories of those transformed, it is evident that the

individual who changes shape is regarded with superstitious reverence, as a being of a higher order—of a
divine nature.   In Christian countries, everything
relating to heathen mythology was regarded with a sus-
picious eye by the clergy, and any miraculous powers
not sanctioned by the church were attributed to the evil
one.   The heathen gods became devils, and the marvels
related of them were supposed to be effected by diabolic
agency.   A case of transformation which had shown the
power of an ancient god, was in Christian times considered as an instance of witchcraft.   Thus stories of
transformation fell into bad odour, and those who
changed shapes were no longer regarded as heavenly
beings, commanding reverence, but as miserable witches
deserving the stake.

In the infancy of the world, when natural phenomena
were ill-understood, expressions which to us are poetical
were of a real significance.   When we speak of thunder
rolling, we use an expression which conveys no further
idea than a certain likeness observed between the detona-
tions and the roll of a vehicle; but to the uninstructed
mind it was more.   The primæval savage knew not what
caused thunder, and tracing the resemblance between it
and the sound of wheels, he at once concluded that the

chariot of the gods was going abroad, or that the celestial
spirits were enjoying a game of bowls.

We speak of fleecy clouds, because they appear to us
soft and light as wool, but the first men tracing the same
resemblance, believed the light vapours to be flocks of
heavenly sheep. Or we say that the clouds are flying:
the savage used the same expression, as he looked up
at the mackerel sky, and saw in it flights of swans
coursing over the heavenly lake. Once more, we creep
nearer to the winter fire, shivering at the wind, which
we remark is howling around the house, and yet we
do not suppose that the wind has a voice. The wild
primæval men thought that it had, and because dogs and
wolves howl, and the wind howled, and because they had
seen dogs and wolves, they concluded that the storm-
wind was a night-hound, or a monstrous wolf, racing
over the country in the darkness of the winter night,
ravening for prey.

Along with the rise of this system of explaining the
operations of nature by analogies in the bestial world,
another conclusion forced itself on the untaught mind.
The flocks which strayed in heaven were no earthly
sheep, but were the property of spiritual beings, and
were themselves perhaps spiritual; the swans which flew

aloft, far above the topmost peak of the Himalaya, were no ordinary swans, but were divine and heavenly. The wolf which howled so wildly in the long winter night, the hounds, whose bay sounded so dismally through the shaking black forest, were no mundane wolves and hounds, but issued from the home of a divine hunter, and were themselves wondrous, supernatural beings of godlike race.

And so, the clouds having become swans, the swan-clouds were next believed to be divine beings, valkyries, apsaras, and the like, seen by mortals in their feather-dresses, but appearing among the gods as damsels. The storm-wind having been supposed to be a wolf, next was taken to be a tempestuous god, who delighted to hunt on earth in lupine form.

I have mentioned also the serpent shape, as being one very favourite in mythology. The ancient people saw the forked and writhing lightning, and supposed it to be a heavenly fiery serpent, a serpent which had god-like powers, which was in fact a divine being, manifesting himself to mortals under that form. Among the North American Indians, the lightning is still regarded as the great serpent, and the thunder is supposed to be his hissing.

" Ah ! " exclaimed a Magdeburg peasant to a German professor, during a thunder-storm, as a vivid forked gleam shot to earth, "what a glorious snake was that ! " And this resemblance did not escape the Greeks.

ἕλικες δ᾽ ἐκλάμπουσι στεροπῆς ζάπυροι.

Æsch. Prom. 1064.

δράκοντα πυρσόνωτον, ὅς ἄπλατον ἀμφελικτὸς
ἕλικ᾽ ἐφρούρει, κτανών.

Eurip. Herc. F. 395.

And according to Aristotle, ἑλικίαι are the light-nings, γραμμοειδῶς φερόμενοι.

It is so difficult for us to unlearn all we know of the nature of meteorological phenomena, so hard for us to look upon atmospheric changes as though we knew nothing of the laws that govern them, that we are disposed to treat such explanations of popular myths as I have given above, as fantastic and improbable.

But among the ancients all solutions of natural problems were tentative, and it is only after the failure of every attempt made to explain these phenomena on supernatural grounds that we have been driven to the discovery of the true interpretation. Yet among the vulgar a vast amount of mythology remains, and is used still to explain atmospheric mysteries. The other day a

Yorkshire girl, when asked why she was not afraid of thunder, replied because it was only her Father's voice; what knew she of the rushing together of air to fill the vacuum caused by the transit of the electric fluid? to her the thunder-clap was the utterance of the Almighty. Still in North Germany does the peasant say of thunder, that the angels are playing skittles aloft, and of the snow, that they are shaking up the feather-beds in heaven.

The myth of the dragon is one which admits, perhaps more than any other, of identification with a meteorological phenomenon, and presents to us as well the phase of transition from theriomorphosis to anthropomorphosis.

The dragon of popular mythology is nothing else than the thunderstorm, rising at the horizon, rushing with expanded, winnowing, black pennons across the sky, darting out its forked fiery tongue, and belching fire. In a Slovakian legend, the dragon sleeps in a mountain cave through the winter months, but, at the equinox, bursts forth—"In a moment the heaven was darkened and became black as pitch, only illumined by the fire which flashed from dragon's jaws and eyes. The earth shuddered, the stones rattled down the mountain sides into the glens. Right and left, left and

right, did the dragon lash his tail, overthrowing pines
and beeches, snapping them as rods.   He evacuated
such floods of water that the mountain torrents were
full. But after a while his power was exhausted, he
lashed no more with his tail, ejected no more water, and
spat no more fire."

I think it is impossible not to see in this description,
a spring-tide thunderstorm.   But to make it more
evident that the untaught mind did regard such a storm
as a dragon, I think the following quotation from *John
of Brompton's Chronicle* will convince the most
sceptical : " Another remarkable thing is this, that took
place during a certain month in the Gulf of Satalia (on
the coast of Pamphylia).   There appeared a great and
black dragon which came in clouds, and let down his
head into the water, whilst his tail seemed turned to
the sky; and the dragon drew the water to him by
drinking, with such avidity, that, if any ship, even
though laden with men or any other heavy articles, had
been near him when drinking, it would nevertheless
have been sucked up and carried on high.   In order
however to avoid this danger, it is necessary, when people
see it, at once to make a great uproar, and to shout and
hammer tables, so that the dragon, hearing the noise,

and the voices of those shouting, may withdraw himself far off. Some people, however, assert that this is not a dragon, but the sun drawing up the waters of the sea; which seems more probable."* Such is John of Brompton's account of a waterspout. In Greek mythology the dragon of the storm has begun to undergo anthropomorphosis. Typhœus is the son of Tartarus and Terra; the storm rising from the horizon may well be supposed to issue from the earth's womb, and its characteristics are sufficient to decide its paternity. Typhœus, the whirlwind or typhoon, has a hundred dragon or serpent heads, the long writhing striæ of vapour which run before the hurricane cloud. He belches fire, that is, lightnings issue from the clouds, and his roaring is like the howling of wild dogs. Typhœus ascends to heaven to make war on the gods, who fly from him in various fantastic shapes; who cannot see in this ascent the hurricane climbing up the vault of sky, and in the flying gods, the many fleeting fragments of white cloud which are seen drifting across the heavens before the gale!

Typhœus, according to Hesiod, is the father of all bad winds, which destroy with rain and tempest, all in

---

* Apud TWYSDEN, *Hist. Anglicæ Script.* x. 1652. p. 1216.

fact which went among the Greeks by the name of
λαῖλαψ, bringing injury to the agriculturist and peril to
the voyager.

> Ἐκ δὲ Τυφωέος ἔστ᾽ ἀνέμων μένος ὑγρὸν ἀέπτων,
> νόσφι Νότου Βορέω τε, καὶ ἀργέστεω Ζεφύρου τε·
> οἵ γε μὲν ἐν θεόφιν γενεή, θνητοῖς μέγ᾽ ὄνειαρ.
> αἱ δ᾽ ἄλλαι μαψαῦραι ἐπιπνείουσι θάλασσαν.
> αἱ δ᾽ ἤτοι πίπτουσαι ἐς ἠεροειδέα πόντον,
> πῆμα μέγα θνητοῖσι, κακῇ θύουσιν ἀέλλῃ.
> ἄλλοτε δ᾽ ἄλλαι ἀείσι, διασκιδνᾶσι τε νῆας,
> ναύτας τε φθείρουσι· κακοῦ δ᾽ οὐ γίγνεται ἀλκὴ
> ἀνδράσιν, οἳ κείνῃσι σινάντωνται κατὰ πόντον·
> αἱ δ᾽ αὖ καὶ κατὰ γαῖαν ἀπείριτον, ἀνθεμόεσσαν,
> ἔργ᾽ ἐρατὰ φθείρουσι χαμαιγενέων ἀνθρώπων,
> πιμπλεῦσαι κόνιός τε καὶ ἀργαλέου κολοσυρτοῦ.
>
> *Hesiod. Theog.* 870, *seq.*

In both modern Greek and Lithuanian household
mythology the dragon or drake has become an ogre, a
gigantic man with few of the dracontine attributes
remaining.   Von Hahn, in his *Griechische und Albanesische Märchen*, tells many tales of drakes, and in all,
the old characteristics have been lost, and the drake is
simply a gigantic man with magical and superhuman
powers.

It is the same among the Lithuanian peasantry.   A
dragon walks on two legs, talks, flirts with a lady, and
marries her.   He retains his evil disposition, but has
sloughed off his scales and wings.

Such is the change which has taken place in the popular conception of the dragon, which is an impersonification of the thunderstorm. A similar change has taken place in the swan-maiden and were-wolf myths.

In ancient Indian Vedaic mythology the apsaras were heavenly damsels who dwelt in the æther, between earth and sun. Their name, which signifies "the shapeless," or "those who go in the water"—it is uncertain which is the correct derivation—is expressive of the white cirrus, constantly changing form, and apparently floating swan-like on the blue heaven-sea. These apsaras, according to the Vedaic creed, were fond of changing their shapes, appearing generally as ducks or swans, occasionally as human beings. The souls of heroes were given to them for lovers and husbands. One of the most graceful of the early Indian myths is the story of the apsaras, Urvaçî. Urvaçî loved Puravaras and became his wife, on the condition that she was never to behold him in a state of nudity. They remained together for years, till the heavenly companions of Urvaçî determined to secure her return to them. They accordingly beguiled Puravaras into leaving his bed in the darkness of night, and then with a lightning flash they disclosed him, in his nudity, to his

wife, who was thereupon constrained to leave him.   He
pursued her, full of sorrow at his loss, and found her
at length swimming in a large lotus pond, in swan's
shape.

That this story is not a mere invention, but rests on
some mythological explanation of natural phenomena, I
think more than probable, as it is found all over the
world with few variations.   As every Aryan branch
retains the story, or traces of it, there can be no doubt
that the belief in swan-maidens, who swam in the
heavenly sea, and who sometimes became the wives of
those fortunate men who managed to steal from them
their feather dresses, formed an integral portion of the
old mythological system of the Aryan family, before it
was broken up into Indian, Persian, Greek, Latin,
Russian, Scandinavian, Teutonic, and other races.   But
more, as the same myth is found in tribes not Aryan,
and far removed from contact with European or Indian
superstition,—as, for instance, among Samoyeds and
American Indians,—it is even possible that this story
may be a tradition of the first primæval stock of
men.

But it is time for me to leave the summer cirrus and
turn to the tempest-born rain-cloud.   It is represented

in ancient Indian mythology by the Vritra or Râkshasas. At first the form of these dæmons was uncertain and obscure. Vritra is often used as an appellative for a cloud, and kabhanda, an old name for a rain-cloud, in later times became the name of a devil. Of Vritra, who envelopes the mountains with vapour, it is said, "The darkness stood retaining the water, the mountains lay in the belly of Vritra." By degrees Vritra stood out more prominently as a dæmon, and he is described as a "devourer" of gigantic proportions. In the same way Râkshasas obtained corporeal form and individuality. He is a misshapen giant "like to a cloud," with a red beard and red hair, with pointed protruding teeth, ready to lacerate and devour human flesh. His body is covered with coarse bristling hair, his huge mouth is open, he looks from side to side as he walks, lusting after the flesh and blood of men, to satisfy his raging hunger, and quench his consuming thirst. Towards nightfall his strength increases manifold. He can change his shape at will. He haunts the woods, and roams howling through the jungle; in short, he is to the Hindoo what the were-wolf is to the European.

A certain wood was haunted by a Râkschasa; he one day came across a Brahmin, and with a bound reached

his shoulders, and clung to them, exclaiming, " Heh !
go on with you ! "   And the Brahmin, quaking with
fear, advanced with him.   But when he observed that
the feet of the Râkschasa were as delicate as the stamens
of the lotus, he asked him, " How is it that you have
such weak and slender feet ? "   The Râkschasa replied,
" I never walk nor touch the earth with my feet.   I have
made a vow not to do so."   Presently they came to a
large pond.   Then the Râkschasa bade the Brahmin
wait at the edge whilst he bathed and prayed to the
gods.   But the Brahmin thought : " As soon as these
prayers and ablutions are over, he will tear me to pieces
with his fangs and eat me.   He has vowed not to walk ;
I will be off post haste ! " so he ran away, and the
Râkschasa dared not follow him for fear of breaking his
vow.   (*Pantschatantra*, v. 13.)   There is a similar
story in the *Mahâbhârata*, xiii., and in the *Kathâ Sarit
Sâgara*, v. 49—53.

I have said sufficient to show that natural phenomena
gave rise to mythological stories, and that these stories
have gradually deteriorated, and have been degraded into
vulgar superstitions.   And I have shown that both the
doctrine of metempsychosis and the mythological explanations of meteorological changes have given rise to

abundant fable, and among others to the popular and wide-spread superstition of lycanthropy. I shall now pass from myth to history, and shall give instances of bloodthirstiness, cruelty, and cannibalism.

CHAPTER XI.

THE MARÉCHAL DE RETZ.—I. THE INVESTIGATION OF CHARGES.

Introduction—History of Gilles de Laval—The Castle of Machecoul—
Surrender of the Marshal—Examination of Witnesses—Letter of
De Retz—The Duke of Brittany reluctant to move—The Bishop of
Nantes.

THE history of the man whose name heads this chapter
I purpose giving in detail, as the circumstances I shall
narrate have, I believe, never before been given with
accuracy to the English public. The name of Gilles
de Laval may be well known, as sketches of his bloody
career have appeared in many biographies, but these
sketches have been very incomplete, as the material
from which they were composed was meagre. M. Michelet
alone ventured to give the public an idea of the crimes
which brought a marshal of France to the gallows, and
his revelations were such that, in the words of M. Henri

Martin, "this iron age, which seemed unable to feel surprise at any amount of evil, was struck with dismay."

M. Michelet derived his information from the abstract of the papers relating to the case, made by order of Ann of Brittany, in the Imperial Library. The original documents were in the library at Nantes, and a great portion of them were destroyed in the Revolution of 1789. But a careful analysis had been made of them, and this valuable abridgment, which was inaccessible to M. Michelet, came into the hands of M. Lacroix, the eminent French antiquarian, who published a memoir of the marshal from the information he had thus obtained, and it is his work, by far the most complete and circumstantial which has appeared, that I condense into the following chapters.

"The most monstrously depraved imagination," says M. Henri Martin, "never could have conceived what the trial reveals." M. Lacroix has been obliged to draw a veil over much that transpired, and I must draw it closer still. I have, however, said enough to show that this memorable trial presents horrors probably unsurpassed in the whole volume of the world's history.

During the year 1440, a terrible rumour spread through Brittany, and especially through the ancient *pays de Retz*, which extends along the south of the Loire from Nantes to Paimbœuf, to the effect that one of the most famous and powerful noblemen in Brittany, Gilles de Laval, Maréchal de Retz, was guilty of crimes of the most diabolical nature.

Gilles de Laval, eldest son of Guy de Laval, second of his name, Sire de Retz, had raised the junior branch of the illustrious house of Laval above the elder branch, which was related to the reigning family of Brittany. He lost his father when he was aged twenty, and remained master of a vast territorial inheritance, which was increased by his marriage with Catharine de Thouars in 1420. He employed a portion of their fortune in the cause of Charles VII., and in strengthening the French crown. During seven consecutive years, from 1426 to 1433, he was engaged in military enterprises against the English; his name is always cited along with those of Dunois, Xaintrailles, Florent d'Illiers, Gaucourt, Richemont, and the most faithful servants of the king. His services were speedily acknowledged by the king creating him Marshal of France. In 1427, he assaulted the Castle of Lude, and carried it by storm; he killed with his own hand the commander of the place; next year he captured from the English the fortress of Rennefort, and the Castle of Malicorne; in 1429, he took an active part in the expedition of Joan of Arc for the deliverance of Orleans, and the occupation of Jargeau, and he was with her in the moat, when she was wounded by an arrow under the walls of Paris.

The marshal, councillor, and chamberlain of the king participated in the direction of public affairs, and soon obtained the entire confidence of his master. He accompanied Charles to Rheims on the occasion of his coronation, and had the honour of bearing the oriflamme, brought for the occasion from the abbey of S. Remi. His intrepidity on the field of battle was as remarkable as his sagacity in council, and he proved himself to be both an excellent warrior and a shrewd politician.

Suddenly, to the surprise of every one, he quitted the service of Charles VII., and sheathed for ever his sword, in the retirement of the country. The death of his maternal grandfather, Jean de Craon, in 1432, made him so enormously wealthy, that his revenues were estimated at 300,000 livres; nevertheless, in two years, by his excessive prodigality, he managed to lose a considerable portion of his inheritance. Mauléon, S. Etienne de Malemort, Loroux-Botereau, Pornic, and Chantolé, he sold to John V., Duke of Brittany, his kinsman, and other lands and seigneurial rights he ceded to the Bishop of Nantes, and to the chapter of the cathedral in that city.

The rumour soon spread that these extensive cessions of territory were sops thrown to the duke and to the bishop, to restrain the one from confiscating his goods, and the other from pronouncing excommunication, for the crimes of which the people whisperingly accused him ; but these rumours were probably without foundation, for eventually it was found hard to persuade the duke of the guilt of his kinsman, and the bishop was the most determined instigator of the trial.

The marshal seldom visited the ducal court, but he often appeared in the city of Nantes, where he inhabited the Hôtel de la Suze, with a princely retinue. He had, always accompanying him, a guard of two hundred men at arms, and a numerous suit of pages, esquires, chaplains, singers, astrologers, &c., all of whom he paid handsomely.

Whenever he left the town, or moved to one of his other seats, the cries of the poor, which had been restrained during the time of his presence, broke forth. Tears flowed, curses were uttered, a long-continued wail rose to heaven, the moment that the last of the marshal's party had left the neighbourhood. Mothers had lost their children, babes had been snatched from the cradle, infants had been spirited away almost from the maternal arms, and it was known by sad experience that the vanished little ones would never be seen again.

But on no part of the country did the shadow of this great fear fall so deeply as on the villages in the neighbourhood of the Castle of Machecoul, a gloomy château, composed of huge towers, and surrounded by deep moats, a residence much frequented by De Retz, notwithstanding its sombre and repulsive appearance. This fortress was always in a condition to resist a siege: the drawbridge was raised, the portcullis down, the gates closed, the men under arms, the culverins on the bastion always loaded. No one, except the servants, had penetrated into this mysterious asylum and had come forth alive. In the surrounding country strange tales of horror and devilry circulated in whispers, and yet it was observed that the chapel of the castle was gorgeously decked with tapestries of silk and cloth of gold, that the sacred vessels were encrusted with gems, and that the vestments of the priests were of the most sumptuous character. The excessive devotion of the marshal was also noticed; he was said to hear mass thrice daily, and to be passionately fond of ecclesiastical music. He was said to have asked permission of the pope, that a crucifer should precede him in processions. But when dusk settled down over the forest, and one by one the windows of the castle became illumined, peasants would point to one casement high up in an isolated tower, from which a clear light streamed through the gloom of night; they spoke of a fierce red glare which irradiated the chamber at times, and of sharp cries ringing out of it, through the hushed woods, to be answered only by the howl of the wolf as it rose from its lair to begin its nocturnal rambles.

On certain days, at fixed hours, the drawbridge sank, and the servants of De Retz stood in the gateway distributing clothes, money, and food to the mendicants who crowded round them soliciting alms. It often happened that children were among the beggars: as often one of the servants would promise them some dainty if they would go to the kitchen for it. Those children who accepted the offer were never seen again.

In 1440 the long-pent-up exasperation of the people

broke all bounds, and with one voice they charged the marshal with the murder of their children, whom they said he had sacrificed to the devil.

This charge came to the ears of the Duke of Brittany, but he pooh-poohed it, and would have taken no steps to investigate the truth, had not one of his nobles insisted on his dôing so. At the same time Jean de Châteaugiron, bishop of Nantes, and the noble and sage Pierre de l'Hospital, grand-seneschal of Brittany, wrote to the duke, expressing very decidedly their views, that the charge demanded thorough investigation.

John V., reluctant to move against a relation, a man who had served his country so well, and was in such a high position, at last yielded to their request, and authorized them to seize the persons of the Sire de Retz and his accomplices. A *serjent d'armes*, Jean Labbé, was charged with this difficult commission. He picked a band of resolute fellows, twenty in all, and in the middle of September they presented themselves at the gate of the castle, and summoned the Sire de Retz to surrender. As soon as Gilles heard that a troop in the livery of Brittany was at the gate, he inquired who was their leader? On receiving the answer "Labbé," he started, turned pale, crossed himself, and prepared to surrender, observing that it was impossible to resist fate.

Years before, one of his astrologers had assured him that he would one day pass into the hands of an Abbé, and, till this moment, De Retz had supposed that the prophecy signified that he should eventually become a monk.

Gilles de Sillé, Roger de Briqueville, and other of the accomplices of the marshal, took to flight, but Henriet and Pontou remained with him.

The drawbridge was lowered and the marshal offered his sword to Jean Labbé. The gallant serjeant approached, knelt to the marshal, and unrolled before him a parchment sealed with the seal of Brittany.

" Tell me the tenor of this parchment ? " said Gilles de Retz with dignity.

" Our good Sire of Brittany enjoins you, my lord, by these presents, to follow me to the good town of Nantes, there to clear yourself of certain criminal charges brought against you."

" I will follow immediately, my friend, glad to obey the will of my lord of Brittany : but, that it may not be said that the Seigneur de Retz has received a mes-

sage without largess, I order my treasurer, Henriet,
to hand over to you and your followers twenty gold
crowns."

"Grand-merci, monseigneur! I pray God that he
may give you good and long life."

"Pray God only to have mercy upon me, and to
pardon my sins."

The marshal had his horses saddled, and left
Machecoul with Pontou and Henriet, who had thrown
in their lot with him.

It was with lively emotion that the people in the
villages traversed by the little troop, saw the redoubted
Gilles de Laval ride through their streets, surrounded by
soldiers in the livery of the Duke of Brittany, and
unaccompanied by a single soldier of his own. The
roads and streets were thronged, peasants left the fields,
women their kitchens, labourers deserted their cattle at
the plough, to throng the road to Nantes. The caval-
cade proceeded in silence. The very crowd which had
gathered to see it, was hushed. Presently a shrill
woman's voice was raised:—

"My child! restore my child!"

Then a wild, wrathful howl broke from the lips of
the throng, rang along the Nantes road, and only died

away, as the great gates of the Château de Bouffay closed on the prisoner.

The whole population of Nantes was in commotion, and it was said that the investigation would be fictitious, that the duke would screen his kinsman, and that the object of general execration would escape with the surrender of some of his lands.

And such would probably have been the event of the trial, had not the Bishop of Nantes and the grand-seneschal taken a very decided course in the matter. They gave the duke no peace till he had yielded to their demand for a thorough investigation and a public trial.

John V. nominated Jean de Toucheronde to collect information, and to take down the charges brought against the marshal. At the same time he was given to understand that the matter was not to be pressed, and that the charges upon which the marshal was to be tried were to be softened down as much as possible.

The commissioner, Jean de Toucheronde, opened the investigation on the 18th September, assisted only by his clerk, Jean Thomas. The witnesses were introduced either singly, or in groups, if they were relations. On entering, the witness knelt before the commissioner, kissed the crucifix, and swore with his hand on the Gospels that he would speak the truth, and nothing but the truth : after this he related all the facts referring to the charge, which came under his cognizance, without being interrupted or interrogated.

The first to present herself was Perrine Loessard, living at la Roche-Bernard.

She related, with tears in her eyes, that two years ago, in the month of September, the Sire de Retz had passed with all his retinue through la Roche-Bernard, on his way from Vannes, and had lodged with Jean Collin. She lived opposite the house in which the nobleman was staying.

Her child, the finest in the village, a lad aged ten, had attracted the notice of Pontou, and perhaps of the marshal himself, who stood at a window, leaning on his squire's shoulder.

Pontou spoke to the child, and asked him whether he would like to be a chorister; the boy replied that his ambition was to be a soldier.

"Well, then," said the squire, "I will equip you."

The lad then laid hold of Pontou's dagger, and expressed his desire to have such a weapon in his belt. Thereupon the mother had run up and had made him leave hold of the dagger, saying that the boy was doing very well at school, and was getting on with his letters, for he was one day to be a monk. Pontou had dissuaded her from this project, and had proposed to take the child with him to Machecoul, and to educate him to be a soldier. Thereupon he had paid her down a hundred sols to buy the lad a dress, and had obtained permission to carry him off.

Next day her son had been mounted on a horse purchased for him from Jean Collin, and had left the village in the retinue of the Sire de Retz. The poor mother at parting had gone in tears to the marshal, and had entreated him to be kind to her child. From that time she had been able to obtain no information regarding her son. She had watched the Sire de Retz whenever he had passed through La Roche Bernard, but had never observed her child among his pages. She had questioned several of the marshal's people, but they had laughed at her; the only answer she had obtained was: "Be not afraid. He is either at Machecoul, or else at Tiffauges, or else at Pornic, or somewhere." Perrine's story was corroborated by Jean Collin, his wife, and his mother-in-law.

Jean Lemegren and his wife, Alain Dulix, Perrot

Duponest, Guillaume Guillon, Guillaume Portayer, Etienne de Monclades, and Jean Lefebure, all inhabitants of S. Etienne de Montluc, deposed that a little child, son of Guillaume Brice of the said parish, having lost his father at the age of nine, lived on alms, and went round the country begging.

This child, named Jamet, had vanished suddenly at midsummer, and nothing was known of what had become of him; but strong suspicions were entertained of his having been carried off by an aged hag who had appeared shortly before in the neighbourhood, and who had vanished along with the child.

On the 27th September, Jean de Toucheronde, assisted by Nicolas Chateau, notary of the court at Nantes, received the depositions of several inhabitants of Pont-de-Launay, near Bouvron : to wit, Guillaume Fourage and wife; Jeanne, wife of Jean Leflou; and Richarde, wife of Jean Gandeau.

These depositions, though very vague, afforded sufficient cause for suspicion to rest on the marshal. Two years before, a child of twelve, son of Jean Bernard, and another child of the same age, son of Ménégué, had gone to Machecoul. The son of Ménégué had returned alone in the evening, relating that his companion had asked him to wait for him on the road whilst he begged at the gates of the Sire de Retz. The son of Ménégué said that he had waited three hours, but his companion had not returned. The wife of Guillaume Fourage deposed that she had seen the lad at this time with an old hag, who was leading him by the hand towards Machecoul. That same evening this hag passed over the bridge of Launay, and the wife of Fourage asked her what had become of little Bernard. The old woman neither stopped nor answered further than by saying he was well provided for. The boy had not been seen since. On the 28th September, the Duke of Brittany joined another commissioner, Jean Couppegorge, and a second notary, Michel Estallure, to Toucheronde and Chateau.

The inhabitants of Machecoul, a little town over which the Sire de Retz exercised supreme power, appeared now to depose against their lord. André Barbier, shoemaker, declared that last Easter, a child, son of his neighbour Georges Lebarbier, had disappeared. He was last seen gathering plums behind the hotel Rondeau. This disappearance surprised none in Machecoul, and no one ventured to comment on it. André and his wife were in daily terror of losing their own child. They had been a pilgrimage to S. Jean d'Angely, and had been asked there whether it was the custom at Machecoul to eat children. On their return they had heard of two children having vanished—the son of Jean Gendron, and that of Alexandre Châtellier. André Barbier had made some inquiries about the circumstances of their disappearance, and had been advised to hold his tongue, and to shut his ears and eyes, unless he were prepared to be thrown into a dungeon by the lord of Machecoul.

"But, bless me!" he had said, "am I to believe that a fairy spirits off and eats our little ones?"

"Believe what you like," was the advice given to him; "but ask no questions." As this conversation had taken place, one of the marshal's men at arms had passed, when all those who had been speaking took to their heels. André, who had run with the rest, without knowing exactly why he fled, came upon a man near the church of the Holy Trinity, who was weeping bitterly, and crying out,—"O my God, wilt Thou not restore to me my little one?" This man had also been robbed of his child.

Licette, wife of Guillaume Sergent, living at La Boncardière, in the parish of S. Croix de Machecoul, had lost her son two years before, and had not seen him since; she besought the commissioners, with tears in her eyes, to restore him to her.

"I left him," said she, "at home whilst I went into the field with my husband to sow flax. He was a bonny little lad, and he was as good as he was bonny. He had to look after his tiny sister, who was a year and a half old. On my return home, the little girl was found, but she could not tell me what had become of him. Afterwards we found in the marsh a small red woollen cap which had belonged to my poor darling; but it was in vain that we dragged the marsh, nothing was found more, except good evidence that he had not been drowned. A hawker who sold needles and thread passed through Machecoul at the time, and told me that an old woman in grey, with a black hood on her head, had bought of him some children's toys, and had a few moments after passed him, leading a little boy by the hand."

Georges Lebarbier, living near the gate of the châtelet de Machecoul, gave an account of the manner in which his son had evanesced. The boy was apprenticed to Jean Pelletier, tailor to Mme. de Retz and to the household of the castle. He seemed to be getting on in his profession, when last year, about S. Barnabas'

day, he went to play at ball on the castle green. He
never returned from the game.

This youth and his master, Jean Pelletier, had been
in the habit of eating and drinking at the castle, and
had always laughed at the ominous stories told by the
people.

Guillaume Hilaire and his wife confirmed the statements of Lebarbier. They also said that they knew of
the loss of the sons of Jean Gendron, Jeanne Rouen,
and Alexandre Châtellier. The son of Jean Gendron,
aged twelve, lived with the said Hilaire and learned of
him the trade of skinner. He had been working in the
shop for seven or eight years, and was a steady, hard-
working lad. One day Messieurs Gilles de Sillé and
Roger de Briqueville entered the shop to purchase a
pair of hunting gloves. They asked if little Gendron
might take a message for them to the castle. Hilaire
readily consented, and the boy received beforehand the
payment for going—a gold angelus, and he started, promising to be back directly. But he had never returned.
That evening Hiliare and his wife, observing Gilles de
Sillé and Roger de Briqueville returning to the castle,
ran to them and asked what had become of the appren-
tice. They replied that they had no notion of where

he was, as they had been absent hunting, but that it was possible he might have been sent to Tiffauges, another castle of De Retz.

Guillaume Hilaire, whose depositions were more grave and explicit than the others, positively asserted that Jean Dujardin, valet to Roger de Briqueville had told him he knew of a cask secreted in the castle, full of children's corpses. He said that he had often heard people say that children were enticed to the château and then murdered, but had treated it as an idle tale. He said, moreover, that the marshal was not accused of having any hand in the murders, but that his servants were supposed to be guilty.

Jean Gendron himself deposed to the loss of his son, and he added that his was not the only child which had vanished mysteriously at Machecoul. He knew of thirty that had disappeared.

Jean Chipholon, elder and junior, Jean Aubin, and Clement Doré, all inhabitants of the parish of Thomage, deposed that they had known a poor man of the same parish, named Mathelin Thomas, who had lost his son, aged twelve, and that he had died of grief in consequence.

Jeanne Rouen, of Machecoul, who for nine years

had been in a state of uncertainty whether her son were
alive or dead, deposed that the child had been carried
off whilst keeping sheep. She had thought that he had
been devoured of wolves, but two women of Machecoul,
now deceased, had seen Gilles de Sillé approach the little
shepherd, speak to him, and point to the castle. Shortly
after the lad had walked off in that direction. The
husband of Jeanne Rouen went to the château to in-
quire after his son, but could obtain no information.
When next Gilles de Sillé appeared in the town, the
disconsolate mother entreated him to restore her child
to her. Gilles replied that he knew nothing about him,
as he had been to the king at Amboise.

Jeanne, widow of Aymery Hedelin, living at Machecoul, had also lost, eight years before, a little child as
he had pursued some butterflies into the wood. At the
same time four other children had been carried off,
those of Gendron, Rouen, and Macé Sorin. She said
that the story circulated through the country was, that
Gilles de Sillé stole children to make them over to the
English, in order to obtain the ransom of his brother
who was a captive. But she added that this report was
traced to the servants of Sillé, and that it was propagated
by them.

One of the last children to disappear was that of Noël Aise, living in the parish of S. Croix.

A man from Tiffauges had said to her (Jeanne Hedelin) that for one child stolen at Machecoul, there were seven carried away at Tiffauges.

Macé Sorin confirmed the deposition of the widow Hedelin, and repeated the circumstances connected with the loss of the children of Châtellier, Rouen, Gendron, and Lebarbier.

Perrine Rondeau had entered the castle with the company of Jean Labbé. She had entered a stable, and had found a heap of ashes and powder, which had a sickly and peculiar smell. At the bottom of a trough she had found a child's shirt covered with blood.

Several inhabitants of the bourg of Fresnay, to wit, Perrot, Parqueteau, Jean Soreau, Catherine Degrépie, Gilles Garnier, Perrine Viellard, Marguerite Rediern, Marie Carfin, Jeanne Laudais, said that they had heard Guillaume Hamelin, last Easter, lamenting the loss of two children.

Isabeau, wife of Guillaume Hamelin, confirmed these depositions, saying that she had lost them seven years before. She had at that time four children; the eldest aged fifteen, the youngest aged seven, went together to Machecoul to buy some bread, but they did not return. She sat up for them all night and next morning. She heard that another child had been lost, the son of Michaut Bonnel of S. Ciré de Retz.

Guillemette, wife of Michaut Bonnel, said that her son had been carried off whilst guarding cows.

Guillaume Rodigo and his wife, living at Bourg-neuf-en-Retz, deposed that on the eve of last S. Bartholomew's day, the Sire de Retz lodged with Guillaume Plumet in his village.

Pontou, who accompanied the marshal, saw a lad of fifteen, named Bernard Lecanino, servant to Rodigo, standing at the door of his house. The lad could not speak much French, but only bas-Breton. Pontou beckoned to him and spoke to him in a low tone. That evening, at ten o'clock, Bernard left his master's house, Rodigo and his wife being absent. The servant maid, who saw him go out, called to him that the supper table was not yet cleared, but he paid no attention to what she said. Rodigo, annoyed at the loss of his servant, asked some of the marshal's men what had become of him. They replied mockingly that they knew nothing of the little Breton, but that he had probably been sent to Tiffauges to be trained as page to their lord.

Marguerite Sorain, the chambermaid alluded to above, confirmed the statement of Rodigo, adding that Pontou had entered the house and spoken with Bernard. Guillaume Plumet and wife confirmed what Rodigo and Sorain had said.

Thomas Aysée and wife deposed to the loss of their son, aged ten, who had gone to beg at the gate of the castle of Machecoul; and a little girl had seen him drawn by an offer of meat into the château.

Jamette, wife of Eustache Drouet of S. Léger, had sent two sons, one aged ten, the other seven, to the castle to obtain alms. They had not been seen since.

On the 2nd October the commissioners sat again, and the charges became graver, and the servants of the marshal became more and more implicated.

The disappearance of thirteen other children was substantiated under circumstances throwing strong suspicion on the inmates of the castle. I will not give the details, for they much resemble those of the former depositions. Suffice it to say that before the commissioners closed the inquiry, a herald of the Duke of Brittany in tabard blew three calls on the trumpet, from the steps of the tower of Bouffay, summoning all

who had additional charges to bring against the Sire de
Retz, to present themselves without delay. As no fresh
witnesses arrived, the case was considered to be made
out, and the commissioners visited the duke, with the
information they had collected, in their hands.

The duke hesitated long as to the steps he should
take. Should he judge and sentence a kinsman, the
most powerful of his vassals, the bravest of his captains,
a councillor of the king, a marshal of France?

Whilst still unsettled in his mind as to the course
he should pursue, he received a letter from Gilles de
Retz, which produced quite a different effect from that
which it had been intended to produce.

"MONSIEUR MY COUSIN AND HONOURED SIRE,—

"IT is quite true that I am perhaps the most
detestable of all sinners, having sinned horribly again
and again, yet have I never failed in my religious duties.
I have heard many masses, vespers, &c., have fasted in
Lent and on vigils, have confessed my sins, deplor-
ing them heartily, and have received the blood of our
Lord at least once in the year.

Since I have been languishing in prison, awaiting
your honoured justice, I have been overwhelmed with

incomparable repentance for my crimes, which I am ready to acknowledge and to expiate as is suitable.

" Wherefore I supplicate you, M. my cousin, to give me licence to retire into a monastery, and there to lead a good and exemplary life. I care not into what monastery I am sent, but I intend that all my goods, &c., should be distributed among the poor, who are the members of Jesus Christ on earth . . . . Awaiting your glorious clemency, on which I rely, I pray God our Lord to protect you and your kingdom.

" He who addresses you is in all earthly humility,

" FRIAR GILLES,

" Carmelite in intention."

The duke read this letter to Pierre de l'Hospital, president of Brittany, and to the Bishop of Nantes, who were those most resolute in pressing on the trial. They were horrified at the tone of this dreadful communication, and assured the duke that the case was so clear, and the steps taken had been so decided, that it was impossible for him to allow De Retz to escape trial by such an impious device as he suggested. In the meantime, the bishop and the grand-seneschal had set on foot an investigation at the castle of Machecoul, and had found numerous traces of human remains. But a complete examination could not be made, as the duke was anxious to screen his kinsman as much as possible, and refused to authorize one.

The duke now summoned his principal officers and held a council with them. They unanimously sided with the bishop and de l'Hospital, and when John still hesitated, the Bishop of Nantes rose and said : "Monseigneur, this case is one for the church as much as for your court to take up. Consequently, if your President of Brittany does not bring the case into secular court, by the Judge of heaven and earth! I will cite the author of these execrable crimes to appear before our ecclesiastical tribunal."

The resolution of the bishop compelled the duke to yield, and it was decided that the trial should take its course without let or hindrance.

In the meantime, the unhappy wife of Gilles de Retz, who had been separated from him for some while, and who loathed his crimes, though she still felt for him as her husband, hurried to the duke with her daughter to entreat pardon for the wretched man. But the duke refused to hear her. Thereupon she went to Amboise to intercede with the king for him who had once been his close friend and adviser.

CHAPTER XII.

THE MARÉCHAL DE RETZ.—II. THE TRIAL.

The Appearance of the Marshal—Pierre de l'Hospital—The Requisition—The Trial adjourned—Meeting of the Marshal and his
Servants—The Confession of Henriet—Pontou persuaded to confess all—The adjourned Trial not hurried on—The Hesitation of
the Duke of Brittany.

On the 10th October, Nicolas Chateau, notary of the
duke, went to the Château of Bouffay, to read to the
prisoner the summons to appear in person on the
morrow before Messire de l'Hospital, President of
Brittany, Seneschal of Rennes, and Chief Justice of
the Duchy of Brittany.

The Sire de Retz, who believed himself already a
novice in the Carmelite order, had dressed in white,
and was engaged in singing litanies. When the summons had been read, he ordered a page to give the
notary wine and cake, and then he returned to his
prayers with every appearance of compunction and piety.

On the morrow Jean Labbé and four soldiers conducted him to the hall of justice. He asked for Pontou
and Henriet to accompany him, but this was not permitted.

He was adorned with all his military insignia, as
though to impose on his judges; he had around his
neck massive chains of gold, and several collars of
knightly orders. His costume, with the exception of his
purpoint, was white, in token of his repentance. His
purpoint was of pearl-grey silk, studded with gold stars,
and girded around his waist by a scarlet belt, from which
dangled a poignard in scarlet velvet sheath. His collar,
cuffs, and the edging of his purpoint were of white
ermine, his little round cap or *chapel* was white,
surrounded with a belt of ermine—a fur which only
the great feudal lords of Brittany had a right to wear.
All the rest of his dress, to the shoes which were long
and pointed, was white.

No one at a first glance would have thought the Sire
de Retz to be by nature so cruel and vicious as he was
supposed to be. On the contrary, his physiognomy
was calm and phlegmatic, somewhat pale, and expressive
of melancholy. His hair and moustache were light
brown, and his beard was clipped to a point. This

beard, which resembled no other beard, was black, but under certain lights it assumed a blue hue, and it was this peculiarity which obtained for the Sire de Retz the surname of Blue-beard, a name which has attached to him in popular romance, at the same time that his story has undergone strange metamorphoses.

But on closer examination of the countenance of Gilles de Retz, contraction in the muscles of the face, nervous quivering of the mouth, spasmodic twitchings of the brows, and above all, the sinister expression of the eyes, showed that there was something strange and frightful in the man. At intervals he ground his teeth like a wild beast preparing to dash upon his prey, and then his lips became so contracted, as they were drawn in and glued, as it were, to his teeth, that their very colour was indiscernible.

At times also his eyes became fixed, and the pupils dilated to such an extent, with a sombre fire quivering in them, that the iris seemed to fill the whole orbit, which became circular, and sank back into the head. At these moments his complexion became livid and cadaverous; his brow, especially just over the nose, was covered with deep wrinkles, and his beard appeared to bristle, and to assume its bluish hues. But, after a few moments, his features became again serene, with a sweet smile reposing upon them, and his expression relaxed into a vague and tender melancholy.

"Messires," said he, saluting his judges, "I pray you to expedite my matter, and despatch as speedily as possible my unfortunate case; for I am peculiarly anxious to consecrate myself to the service of God, who has pardoned my great sins. I shall not fail, I assure you, to endow several of the churches in Nantes, and I shall distribute the greater portion of my goods among the poor, to secure the salvation of my soul."

"Monseigneur," replied gravely Pierre de l'Hospital: "It is always well to think of the salvation of one's soul; but, if you please, think now that we are concerned with the salvation of your body."

"I have confessed to the father superior of the Carmelites," replied the marshal, with tranquillity; "and through his absolution I have been able to communicate : I am, therefore, guiltless and purified."

"Men's justice is not in common with that of God, monseigneur, and I cannot tell you what will be your sentence. Be ready to make your defence, and listen to the charges brought against you, which M. le Lieutenant du Procureur de Nantes will read."

The officer rose, and read the following paper of charges, which I shall condense :—

" Having heard the bitter complaints of several of the inhabitants of the diocese of Nantes, whose names follow hereinafter (here follow the names of the parents of the lost children), we, Philippe de Livron, lieutenant assesseur of Messire le Procureur de Nantes, have invited, and do invite, the very noble and very wise Messire Pierre de l'Hospital, President of Brittany, &c., to bring to trial the very high and very powerful lord, Gilles de Laval, Sire de Retz, Machecoul, Ingrande and other places, Councillor of his Majesty the King, and Marshal of France :

" Forasmuch as the said Sire de Retz has seized and caused to be seized several little children, not only ten or twenty, but thirty, forty, fifty, sixty, one hundred, two hundred, and more, and has murdered and slain them inhumanly, and then burned their bodies to convert them to ashes :

" Forasmuch as persevering in evil, the said Sire, notwithstanding that the powers that be are ordained of God, and that every one should be an obedient subject to his prince, . . . has assaulted Jean Leferon, subject of the Duke of Brittany, the said Jean Leferon being guardian of the fortress of Malemort, in the name of Geoffrey Leferon, his brother, to whom the said lord had made over the possession of the said place:

"Forasmuch as the said Sire forced Jean Leferon to give up to him the said place, and moreover retook the lordship of Malemort in despite of the order of the duke and of justice:

"Forasmuch as the said Sire arrested Master Jean Rousseau, sergeant of the duke, who was sent to him with injunctions from the said duke, and beat his men with their own staves, although their persons were under the protection of his grace:

"We conclude that the said Sire de Retz, homicide in fact and in intent according to the first count, rebel and felon according to the second, should be condemned to suffer corporal punishment, and to pay a fine of his possessions in lands and goods held in fief to the said nobleman, and that these should be confiscated and remitted to the crown of Brittany."

This requisition was evidently drawn up with the view of saving the life of the Sire de Retz; for the crime of homicide was presented without aggravating circumstances, in such a manner that it could be denied or shelved, whilst the crimes of felony and rebellion against the Duke of Brittany were brought into exaggerated prominence.

Gilles de Retz had undoubtedly been forewarned of the course which was to be pursued, and he was prepared to deny totally the charges made in the first count.

"Monseigneur," said Pierre de l'Hospital, whom the form of the requisition had visibly astonished : "What justification have you to make ? Take an oath on the Gospels to declare the truth."

"No, messire !" answered the marshal. "The witnesses are bound to declare what they know upon oath, but the accused is never put on his oath."

"Quite so," replied the judge. " Because the accused may be put on the rack and constrained to speak the truth, an' please you."

Gilles de Retz turned pale, bit his lips, and cast a glance of malignant hate at Pierre de l'Hospital ; then, composing his countenance, he spoke with an appearance of calm :—

"Messires, I shall not deny that I behaved wrongfully in the case of Jean Rousseau ; but, in excuse, let me say that the said Rousseau was full of wine, and he behaved with such indecorum towards me in the presence of my servants, that it was quite intolerable. Nor will I deny my revenge on the brothers Leferon : Jean had declared that the said Grace of Brittany had confiscated my fortress of Malemort, which I had sold to him, and for which I have not yet received payment; and Geoffrey Leferon had announced far and wide that I was about to be expelled Brittany as a traitor and a rebel. To punish them I re-entered my fortress of Malemort.—As for the other charges, I shall say nothing about them, they are simply false and calumnious."

"Indeed!" exclaimed Pierre de l'Hospital, whose blood boiled with indignation against the wretch who stood before him with such effrontery. "All these witnesses who complain of having lost their children, lied under oath!"

"Undoubtedly, if they accuse me of having anything to do with their loss. What am I to know about them, am I their keeper?"

"The answer of Cain!" exclaimed Pierre de l'Hospital, rising from his seat in the vehemence of his emotion. "However, as you solemnly deny these charges, we must question Henriet and Pontou."

"Henriet, Pontou!" cried the marshal, trembling; "they accuse me of nothing, surely!"

"Not as yet, they have not been questioned, but they are about to be brought into court, and I do not expect that they will lie in the face of justice."

"I demand that my servants be not brought forward as witnesses against their master," said the marshal, his eyes dilating, his brow wrinkling, and his beard bristling blue upon his chin: "a master is above the gossiping tales and charges of his servants."

"Do you think then, messire, that your servants will accuse you?"

"I demand that I, a marshal of France, a baron of the duchy, should be sheltered from the slanders of small folk, whom I disown as my servants if they are untrue to their master."

"Messire, I see we must put you on the rack, or nothing will be got from you."

"Hola! I appeal to his grace the Duke of Brittany, and ask an adjournment, that I may take advice on the charges brought against me, which I have denied, and which I deny still."

"Well, I shall adjourn the case till the 25th of this month, that you may be well prepared to meet the accusations."

On his way back to prison, the marshal passed

Henriet and Pontou as they were being conducted to the court. Henriet pretended not to see his master, but Pontou burst into tears on meeting him. The marshal held out his hand, and Pontou kissed it affectionately.

" Remember what I have done for you, and be faithful servants," said Gilles de Retz. Henriet recoiled from him with a shudder, and the marshal passed on.

" I shall speak," whispered Henriet; " for we have another master beside our poor master of Retz, and we shall soon be with the heavenly one."

The president ordered the clerk to read again the requisition of the lieutenant, that the two presumed accomplices of Gilles de Retz might be informed of the charges brought against their master. Henriet burst into tears, trembled violently, and cried out that he would tell all. Pontou, alarmed, tried to hinder his companion, and said that Henriet was touched in his head, and that what he was about to say would be the ravings of insanity.

Silence was imposed upon him.

" I will speak out," continued Henriet; " and yet I dare not speak of the horrors which I know have taken place, before that image of my Lord Christ; " and he

pointed tremblingly to a large crucifix above the seat
of the judge.

"Henriet," moaned Pontou, squeezing his hand,
"you will destroy yourself as well as your master."

Pierre de l'Hospital rose, and the figure of our
Redeemer was solemnly veiled.

Henriet, who had great difficulty in overcoming his
agitation, than began his revelations.

The following is the substance of them : —

On leaving the university of Angers, he had taken
the situation of reader in the house of Gilles de Retz.
The marshal took a liking to him, and made him his
chamberlain and confidant.

On the occasion of the Sire de la Suze, brother of
the Sire de Retz, taking possession of the castle of
Chantoncé, Charles de Soenne, who had arrived at
Chantoncé, assured Henriet that he had found in the
oubliettes of a tower a number of dead children, some
headless, others frightfully mutilated. Henriet then
thought that this was but a calumny invented by the
Sire de la Suze.

But when, some while after, the Sire de Retz
retook the castle of Chantoncé, and had ceded it to the
Duke of Brittany, he one evening summoned Henriet,

Pontou, and a certain Petit Robin to his room; the two latter were already deep in the secrets of their master. But before confiding anything to Henriet, De Retz made him take a solemn oath never to reveal what he was about to tell him. The oath taken, the Sire de Retz, addressing the three, said that on the morrow an officer of the duke would take possession of the castle in the name of the duke, and that it was necessary, before this took place, that a certain well should be emptied of children's corpses, and that their bodies should be put into boxes and transported to Machecoul.

Henriet, Pontou, and Petit Robin went together, furnished with ropes and hooks, to the tower where were the corpses. They toiled all night in removing the half-decayed bodies, and with them they filled three large cases, which they sent by a boat down the Loire to Machecoul, where they were reduced to ashes.

Henriet counted thirty-six children's heads, but there were more bodies than heads. This night's work, he said, had produced a profound impression on his imagination, and he was constantly haunted with a vision of these heads rolling as in a game of skittles, and clashing with a mournful wail.

Henriet soon began to collect children for his master, and was present whilst he massacred them. They were murdered invariably in one room at Machecoul. The marshal used to bathe in their blood; he was fond of making Gilles de Sillé, Pontou, or Henriet torture them, and he experienced intense pleasure in seeing them in their agonies. But his great passion was to welter in their blood. His servants would stab a child in the jugular vein, and let the blood squirt over him. The room was often steeped in blood. When the horrible deed was done, and the child was dead, the marshal would be filled with grief for what he had done, and would toss weeping and praying on a bed, or recite fervent prayers and litanies on his knees, whilst his servants washed the floor, and burned in the huge fireplace the bodies of the murdered children. With the bodies were burned the clothes and everything that had belonged to the little victims.

An insupportable odour filled the room, but the Maréchal de Retz inhaled it with delight.

Henriet acknowledged that he had seen forty children put to death in this manner, and he was able to give an account of several, so that it was possible to identify them with the children reported to be lost.

"It is quite impossible," said the lieutenant, who had been given the cue to do all that was possible to save the marshal—"It is impossible that bodies could be burned in a chamber fireplace."

"It was done, for all that, messire," replied Henriet. "The fireplace was very large, both at the hotel Suze, and also at Machecoul; we piled up great faggots and logs, and laid the dead children among them. In a few hours the operation was complete, and we flung the ashes out of the window into the moat."

Henriet remembered the case of the two sons of Hamelin; he said that, whilst the one child was being tortured, the other was on its knees sobbing and praying to God, till its own turn came.

"What you have said concerning the excesses of Messire de Retz," exclaimed the lieutenant du procureur, "seems to be pure invention, and destitute of all probability. The greatest monsters of iniquity never committed such crimes, except perhaps some Cæsars of old Rome."

"Messire, it was the acts of these Cæsars that my Lord of Retz desired to imitate. I used to read to him the chronicles of Suetonius, and Tacitus, in which their cruelties are recorded. He used to delight in hearing of them, and he said that it gave him greater pleasure to hack off a child's head than to assist at a banquet. Sometimes he would seat himself on the breast of a little one, and with a knife sever the head from the body at a single blow; sometimes he cut the throat half through very gently, that the child might languish, and he would wash his hands and his beard in its blood. Sometimes he had all the limbs chopped off at once from the trunk; at other times he ordered us to hang the infants till they were nearly dead, and then take them down and cut their throats. I remember having brought to him three little girls who were asking charity at the castle gates. He bade me cut their throats whilst he looked on. André Bricket found another little girl crying on the steps of the house at Vannes because she had lost her mother. He brought the little thing —it was but a babe—in his arms to my lord, and it was killed before him. Pontou and I had to make away with the body. We threw it down a privy in one of the towers, but the corpse caught on a nail in the outer wall, so that it would be visible to all who passed. Pontou was let down by a rope, and he disengaged it with great difficulty."

"How many children do you estimate that the Sire de Retz and his servants have killed?"

" The reckoning is long. I, for my part, confess to having killed twelve with my own hand, by my master's orders, and I have brought him about sixty. I knew that things of the kind went on before I was admitted to the secret; for the castle of Machecoul had been occupied a short while by the Sire de la Sage. My lord recovered it speedily, for he knew that there were many children's corpses hidden in a hayloft. There were forty there quite dry and black as coal, because they had been charred. One of the women of Madame de Retz came by chance into the loft and saw the corpses. Roger de Briqueville wanted to kill her, but the maréchal would not let him."

" Have you nothing more to declare ? "

" Nothing. I ask Pontou, my friend, to corroborate what I have said."

This deposition, so circumstantial and detailed, produced on the judges a profound impression of horror. Human imagination at this time had not penetrated such mysteries of refined cruelty. Several times, as Henriet spake, the president had shown his astonishment and indignation by signing himself with the cross. Several times his face had become scarlet, and his eyes had fallen; he had pressed his hand to his brow, to assure himself that he was not labouring under a hideous dream, and a quiver of horror had run through his whole frame.

Pontou had taken no part in the revelation of Henriet; but when the latter appealed to him he raised his head, looked sadly round the court, and sighed.

"Etienne Cornillant, alias Pontou, I command you in the name of God and of justice, to declare what you know."

This injunction of Pierre de l'Hospital remained unresponded to, and Pontou seemed to strengthen himself in his resolution not to accuse his master.

But Henriet, flinging himself into the arms of his accomplice, implored him, as he valued his soul, no longer to harden his heart to the calls of God; but to bring to light the crimes he had committed along with the Sire de Retz.

The lieutenant du procureur, who hitherto had endeavoured to extenuate or discredit the charges brought against Gilles de Retz, tried a last expedient to counterbalance the damaging confessions of Henriet, and to withhold Pontou from giving way.

"You have heard, monseigneur," said he to the president, "the atrocities which have been acknowledged by Henriet, and you, as I do, consider them to be pure inventions of the aforesaid, made out of bitter hatred and envy with the purpose of ruining his master. I therefore demand that Henriet should be put on the rack, that he may be brought to give the lie to his former statements."

"You forget," replied de l'Hospital, "that the rack is for those who do *not* confess, and not for those who freely acknowledge their crimes. Therefore I order the second accused, Etienne Cornillant, alias Pontou, to be placed on the rack if he continues silent. Pontou! will you speak or will you not?"

"Monseigneur, he will speak!" exclaimed Henriet. "Oh, Pontou, dear friend, resist not God any more."

"Well then, messeigneurs," said Pontou, with emotion; "I will satisfy you; I cannot defend my poor lord against the allegations of Henriet, who has confessed all through dread of eternal damnation."

He then fully substantiated all the statements of the other, adding other facts of the same character, known only to himself.

Notwithstanding the avowal of Pontou and Henriet, the adjourned trial was not hurried on. It would have been easy to have captured some of the accomplices of

the wretched man; but the duke, who was informed of
the whole of the proceedings, did not wish to augment
the scandal by increasing the number of the accused.
He even forbade researches to be made in the castles
and mansions of the Sire de Retz, fearing lest proofs of
fresh crimes, more mysterious and more horrible than
those already divulged, should come to light.

The dismay spread through the country by the
revelations already made, demanded that religion and
morality, which had been so grossly outraged, should be
speedily avenged. People wondered at the delay in
pronouncing sentence, and it was loudly proclaimed in
Nantes that the Sire de Retz was rich enough to purchase his life. It is true that Madame de Retz solicited
the king and the duke again to give pardon to her husband; but the duke, counselled by the bishop, refused to
extend his authority to interfere with the course of
justice; and the king, after having sent one of his coun-
cillors to Nantes to investigate the case, determined not
to stir in it.

CHAPTER XIII.

MARÉCHAL DE RETZ.—III. THE SENTENCE AND EXECUTION.

The adjourned Trial—The Marshal Confesses—The Case handed over
to the Ecclesiastical Tribunal—Prompt steps taken by the Bishop
—The Sentence—Ratified by the Secular Court—The Execution.

ON the 24th October the trial of the Maréchal de Retz
was resumed. The prisoner entered in a Carmelite
habit, knelt and prayed in silence before the examination began. Then he ran his eye over the court, and
the sight of the rack, windlass, and cords made a slight
shudder run through him.

"Messire Gilles de Laval," began the president;
"you appear before me now for the second time to
answer to a certain requisition read by M. le Lieutenant
du Procureur de Nantes."

" I shall answer frankly, monseigneur," said the
prisoner calmly; "but I reserve the right of appeal to

the benign intervention of the very venerated majesty
of the King of France, of whom I am, or have been,
chamberlain and marshal, as may be proved by my
letters patent duly enregistered in the parliament at
Paris——"

" This is no affair of the King of France," interrupted Pierre de l'Hospital; "if you were chamberlain
and marshal of his Majesty, you are also vassal of his
grace the Duke of Brittany."

" I do not deny it; but, on the contrary, I trust to
his Grace of Brittany to allow me to retire to a convent
of Carmelites, there to repent me of my sins."

" That is as may be; will you confess, or must I
send you to the rack ? "

" Torture me not ! " exclaimed Gilles de Retz ; " I
will confess all. Tell me first, what have Henriet and
Pontou said ?"

" They have confessed. M. le Lieutenant du Procureur shall read you their allegations."

" Not so," said the lieutenant, who continued to
show favour to the accused ; "I pronounce them false,
unless Messire de Retz confirms them by oath, which
God forbid ! "

Pierre de l'Hospital made a motion of anger to check

this scandalous pleading in favour of the accused, and then nodded to the clerk to read the evidence.

The Sire de Retz, on hearing that his servants had made such explicit avowals of their acts, remained motionless, as though thunderstruck. He saw that it was in vain for him to equivocate, and that he would have to confess all.

"What have you to say?" asked the president, when the confessions of Henriet and Pontou had been read.

"Say what befits you, my lord," interrupted the lieutenant du procureur, as though to indicate to the accused the line he was to take: "are not these abominable lies and calumnies trumped up to ruin you?"

"Alas, no!" replied the Sire de Retz; and his face was pale as death: "Henriet and Pontou have spoken the truth. God has loosened their tongues."

"My lord! relieve yourself of the burden of your crimes by acknowledging them at once," said M. de l'Hospital earnestly.

"Messires!" said the prisoner, after a moment's silence: "it is quite true that I have robbed mothers of their little ones; and that I have killed their

children, or caused them to be killed, either by cutting
their throats with daggers or knives, or by chopping off
their heads with cleavers; or else I have had their skulls
broken by hammers or sticks; sometimes I had their
limbs hewn off one after another; at other times I have
ripped them open, that I might examine their entrails
and hearts; I have occasionally strangled them or put
them to a slow death; and when the children were
dead I had their bodies burned and reduced to ashes."

"When did you begin your execrable practices?"
asked Pierre de l'Hospital, staggered by the frankness
of these horrible avowals: "the evil one must have
possessed you."

"It came to me from myself,—no doubt at the
instigation of the devil: but still these acts of cruelty
afforded me incomparable delight. The desire to commit these atrocities came upon me eight years ago. I
left court to go to Chantoncé, that I might claim the
property of my grandfather, deceased. In the library of
the castle I found a Latin book—*Suetonius*, I believe—
full of accounts of the cruelties of the Roman Emperors.
I read the charming history of Tiberius, Caracalla, and
other Cæsars, and the pleasure they took in watching
the agonies of tortured children. Thereupon I resolved

to imitate and surpass these same Cæsars, and that very night I began to do so. For some while I confided my secret to no one, but afterwards I communicated it to my cousin, Gilles de Sillé, then to Master Roger de Briqueville, next in succession to Henriet, Pontou, Rossignol, and Robin." He then confirmed all the accounts given by his two servants. He confessed to about one hundred and twenty murders in a single year.

"An average of eight hundred in less than seven years!" exclaimed Pierre de l'Hospital, with a cry of pain: "Ah! messire, you were possessed!"

His confession was too explicit and circumstantial for the Lieutenant du Procureur to say another word in his defence; but he pleaded that the case should be made over to the ecclesiastical court, as there were confessions of invocations of the devil and of witchcraft mixed up with those of murder. Pierre de l'Hospital saw that the object of the lieutenant was to gain time for Mme. de Retz to make a fresh attempt to obtain a pardon; however he was unable to resist, so he consented that the case should be transferred to the bishop's court.

But the bishop was not a man to let the matter

slip, and there and then a sergeant of the bishop summoned Gilles de Laval, Sire de Retz, to appear forthwith before the ecclesiastical tribunal. The marshal was staggered by this unexpected citation, and he did not think of appealing against it to the president; he merely signed his readiness to follow, and he was at once conducted into the ecclesiastical court assembled hurriedly to try him.

This new trial lasted only a few hours.

The marshal, now thoroughly cowed, made no attempt to defend himself, but he endeavoured to bribe the bishop into leniency, by promises of the surrender of all his lands and goods to the Church, and begged to be allowed to retire into the Carmelite monastery at Nantes.

His request was peremptorily refused, and sentence of death was pronounced against him.

On the 25th October, the ecclesiastical court having pronounced judgment, the sentence was transmitted to the secular court, which had now no pretext upon which to withhold ratification.

There was some hesitation as to the kind of death the marshal was to suffer. The members of the secular tribunal were not unanimous on this point. The president put it to the vote, and collected the votes himself; then he reseated himself, covered his head, and said in a solemn voice : —

" The court, notwithstanding the quality, dignity, and nobility of the accused, condemns him to be hung and burned. Wherefore I admonish you who are condemned, to ask pardon of God, and grace to die well, in great contrition for having committed the said crimes. And the said sentence shall be carried into execution to-morrow morning between eleven and twelve o'clock." A similar sentence was pronounced upon Henriet and Pontou.

On the morrow, October 26th, at nine o'clock in the morning, a general procession composed of half the people of Nantes, the clergy and the bishop bearing the blessed Sacrament, left the cathedral and went round the city visiting each of the principal churches, where masses were said for the three under sentence.

At eleven the prisoners were conducted to the place of execution, which was in the meadow of Biesse, on the further side of the Loire.

Three gibbets had been erected, one higher than the others, and beneath each was a pile of faggots, tar, and brushwood.

It was a glorious, breezy day, not a cloud was to be seen in the blue heavens; the Loire rolled silently towards the sea its mighty volumes of turbid water, seeming bright and blue as it reflected the brilliancy and colour of the sky. The poplars shivered and whitened in the fresh air with a pleasant rustle, and the willows flickered and wavered above the stream.

A vast crowd had assembled round the gallows; it was with difficulty that a way was made for the condemned, who came on chanting the *De profundis*. The spectators of all ages took up the psalm and chanted it with them, so that the surge of the old Gregorian tone might have been heard by the duke and the bishop, who had shut themselves up in the château of Nantes during the hour of execution.

After the close of the psalm, which was terminated by the *Requiem æternam* instead of the *Gloria*, the Sire de Retz thanked those who had conducted him, and then embraced Pontou and Henriet, before delivering himself of the following address, or rather sermon :—

"My very dear friends and servants, be strong and courageous against the assaults of the devil, and feel great displeasure and contrition for your ill deeds, without despairing of God's mercy. Believe with me,

that there is no sin, however great, in the world, which
God, in his grace and loving kindness, will not pardon,
when one asks it of Him with contrition of heart.
Remember that the Lord God is always more ready to
receive the sinner than is the sinner to ask of Him
pardon.   Moreover, let us very humbly thank Him for his
great love to us in letting us die in full possession of our
faculties, and not cutting us off suddenly in the midst of
our misdeeds.   Let us conceive such a love of God, and
such repentance, that we shall not fear death, which is
only a little pang, without which we could not see God
in his glory.   Besides we must desire to be freed from
this world, in which is only misery, that we may go to
everlasting glory.   Let us rejoice rather, for although
we have sinned grievously here below, yet we shall be
united in Paradise, our souls being parted from our
bodies, and we shall be together for ever and ever, if
only we endure in our pious and honourable contrition
to our last sigh." *   Then the marshal, who was to be
executed first, left his companions and placed himself in

---

* The case of the Sire de Retz is one to make us see the great
danger there is in trusting to feelings in matters of religion. " If thou
wilt enter into life, keep the commandments," said our Lord. How
many hope to go to heaven because they have pious emotions!

the hands of his executioners. He took off his cap, knelt, kissed a crucifix, and made a pious oration to the crowd much in the style of his address to his friends Pontou and Henriet.

Then he commenced reciting the prayers of the dying; the executioner passed the cord round his neck, and adjusted the knot. He mounted a tall stool, erected at the foot of the gallows as a last honour paid to the nobility of the criminal. The pile of firewood was lighted before the executioners had left him.

Pontou and Henriet, who were still on their knees, raised their eyes to their master and cried to him, extending their arms,—

"At this last hour, monseigneur, be a good and valiant soldier of God, and remember the passion of Jesus Christ which wrought our redemption. Farewell, we hope soon to meet in Paradise!"

The stool was cast down, and the Sire de Retz dropped. The fire roared up, the flames leaped about him, and enveloped him as he swung.

Suddenly, mingling with the deep booming of the cathedral bell, swelled up the wild unearthly wail of the *Dies iræ*.

No sound among the crowd, only the growl of the fire, and the solemn strain of the hymn :—

> Lo, the Book, exactly worded,
> Wherein all hath been recorded;
> Thence shall judgment be awarded.
>
> When the Judge his seat attaineth,
> And each hidden deed arraigneth,
> Nothing unavenged remaineth.
>
> What shall I, frail man, be pleading?
> Who for me be interceding?
> When the just are mercy needing.
>
> King of Majesty tremendous,
> Who dost free salvation send us,
> Fount of pity! then befriend us.
>
> *   *   *   *
>
> Low I kneel, with heart-submission;
> See, like ashes, my contrition—
> Help me in my last condition!
>
> Ah! that day of tears and mourning!
> From the dust of earth returning,
> Man for judgment must prepare him!
> Spare, O God, in mercy spare him!
> Lord, who didst our souls redeem,
> Grant a blessed requiem!
>
> AMEN.

Six women, veiled, and robed in white, and six Carmelites advanced bearing a coffin.

It was whispered that one of the veiled women was

Madame de Retz, and that the others were members of the most illustrious houses of Brittany.

The cord by which the marshal was hung was cut, and he fell into a cradle of iron prepared to receive the corpse. The body was removed before the fire had gained any mastery over it. It was placed in the coffin, and the monks and the women transported it to the Carmelite monastery of Nantes, according to the wishes of the deceased.

In the meantime, the sentence had been executed upon Pontou and Henriet; they were hung and burned to dust. Their ashes were cast to the winds; whilst in the Carmelite church of Our Lady were celebrated with pomp the obsequies of the very high, very powerful, very illustrious Seigneur Gilles de Laval, Sire de Retz, late Chamberlain of King Charles VII., and Marshal of France!

CHAPTER XIV.

A GALICIAN WERE-WOLF.

The Inhabitants of Austrian Galicia—The Hamlet of Polomyja—
Summer Evening in the Forest—The Beggar Swiatek—A Girl
disappears—A School-boy vanishes—A Servant-girl lost—Another
Boy carried off—The Discovery made by the Publican of Polomyja
—Swiatek locked up—Brought to Dabkow—Commits Suicide.

THE inhabitants of Austrian Galicia are quiet, inoffensive
people, take them as a whole. The Jews, who number
a twelfth of the population, are the most intelligent,
energetic, and certainly the most money-making individuals in the province, though the Poles proper, or
Mazurs, are not devoid of natural parts.

Perhaps as remarkable a phenomenon as any other
in that kingdom—for kingdom of Waldimir it was—is
the enormous numerical preponderance of the nobility
over the untitled. In 1837 the proportions stood thus:
32,190 nobles to 2,076 tradesmen.

The average of execution for crime is nine a year, out of a population of four and a half millions,—by no means a high figure, considering the peremptory way in which justice is dealt forth in that province. Yet, in the most quiet and well-disposed neighbourhoods, occasionally the most startling atrocities are committed, occurring when least expected, and sometimes perpetrated by the very person who is least suspected.

Just sixteen years ago there happened in the circle of Tornow, in Western Galicia—the province is divided into nine circles—a circumstance which will probably furnish the grandames with a story for their firesides, during their bitter Galician winters, for many a long year.

In the circle of Tornow, in the lordship of Parkost, is a little hamlet called Polomyja, consisting of eight hovels and a Jewish tavern. The inhabitants are mostly woodcutters, hewing down the firs of the dense forest in which their village is situated, and conveying them to the nearest water, down which they are floated to the Vistula. Each tenant pays no rent for his cottage and patch of field, but is bound to work a fixed number of days for his landlord: a practice universal in Galicia, and often productive of much discontent and injustice, as the proprietor exacts labour from his tenant on those days when the harvest has to be got in, or the land is in best condition for tillage, and just when the peasant would gladly be engaged upon his own small plot. Money is scarce in the province, and this is accordingly the only way in which the landlord can be sure of his dues.

Most of the villagers of Polomyja are miserably poor; but by cultivating a little maize, and keeping a few fowls or a pig, they scrape together sufficient to sustain life. During the summer the men collect resin from the pines, from each of which, once in twelve years, they strip a slip of bark, leaving the resin to exude and trickle into a small earthenware jar at its roots; and, during the winter, as already stated, they fell the trees and roll them down to the river.

Polomyja is not a cheerful spot—nested among dense masses of pine, which shed a gloom over the little hamlet; yet, on a fine day, it is pleasant enough for the old women to sit at their cottage doors, scenting that matchless pine fragrance, sweeter than the balm of the Spice Islands, for there is nothing cloying in that exquisite and exhilarating odour; listening to the harp-like thrill of the breeze in the old grey tree-tops, and knitting quietly at long stockings, whilst their little grandchildren romp in the heather and tufted fern.

Towards evening, too, there is something indescribably beautiful in the firwood. The sun dives among the trees, and paints their boles with patches of luminous saffron, or falling over a level clearing, glorifies it with its orange dye, so visibly contrasting with the blue-purple shadow on the western rim of unreclaimed forest, deep and luscious as the bloom on a plum. The birds then are hastening to their nests, a ger-falcon, high overhead, is kindled with sunlight; capering and gambolling among the branches, the merry squirrel skips home for the night.

The sun goes down, but the sky is still shining with twilight. The wild cat begins to hiss and squall in the forest, the heron to flap hastily by, the stork on the top of the tavern chimney to poise itself on one leg for sleep. To-whoo! an owl begins to wake up. Hark! the wood-cutters are coming home with a song.

Such is Polomyja in summer time, and much resembling it are the hamlets scattered about the forest, at intervals of a few miles; in each, the public-house being the most commodious and best-built edifice, the church, whenever there is one, not remarkable for anything but its bulbous steeple.

You would hardly believe that amidst all this poverty a beggar could have picked up any subsistence, and yet, a few years ago, Sunday after Sunday, there sat a white-bearded venerable man at the church door, asking alms.

Poor people are proverbially compassionate and liberal, so that the old man generally got a few coppers, and often some good woman bade him come into her cottage, and let him have some food.

Occasionally Swiatek—that was the beggar's name, went his rounds selling small pinchbeck ornaments and beads; generally, however, only appealing to charity.

One Sunday, after church, a Mazur and his wife invited the old man into their hut and gave him a crust of pie and some meat. There were several children about, but a little girl, of nine or ten, attracted the old man's attention by her artless tricks.

Swiatek felt in his pocket and produced a ring, enclosing a piece of coloured glass set over foil. This he presented to the child, who ran off delighted to show her acquisition to her companions.

"Is that little maid your daughter?" asked the beggar.

" No," answered the house-wife, " she is an orphan; there was a widow in this place who died, leaving the child, and I have taken charge of her; one mouth more will not matter much, and the good God will bless us."

" Ay, ay! to be sure He will; the orphans and fatherless are under His own peculiar care."

" She's a good little thing, and gives no trouble," observed the woman. " You go back to Polomyja to-night, I reckon."

" I do—ah!" exclaimed Swiatek, as the little girl ran up to him. " You like the ring, is it not beautiful? I found it under a big fir to the left of the churchyard,— there may be dozens there. You must turn round three times, bow to the moon, and say, ' Zaboï! ' then look among the tree-roots till you find one."

" Come along!" screamed the child to its comrades; " we will go and look for rings."

" You must seek separately," said Swiatek.

The children scampered off into the wood.

" I have done one good thing for you," laughed the beggar, " in ridding you, for a time, of the noise of those children."

" I am glad of a little quiet now and then," said the

woman; "the children will not let the baby sleep at times with their clatter. Are you going?"

"Yes; I must reach Polomyja to-night. I am old and very feeble, and poor "—he began to fall into his customary whine—" very poor, but I thank and pray to God for you."

Swiatek left the cottage.

That little orphan was never seen again.

The Austrian Government has, of late years, been vigorously advancing education among the lower orders, and establishing schools throughout the province.

The children were returning from class one day, and were scattered among the trees, some pursuing a field-mouse, others collecting juniper-berries, and some sauntering with their hands in their pockets, whistling.

"Where's Peter?" asked one little boy of another who was beside him. "We three go home the same way, let us go together."

"Peter!" shouted the lad.

"Here I am!" was the answer from among the trees; "I'll be with you directly."

"Oh, I see him!" said the elder boy. "There is some one talking to him."

"Where?"

"Yonder, among the pines. Ah! they have gone further into the shadow, and I cannot see them any more. I wonder who was with him; a man, I think."

The boys waited till they were tired, and then they sauntered home, determined to thrash Peter for having kept them waiting. *But Peter was never seen again.*

Some time after this a servant-girl, belonging to a small store kept by a Russian, disappeared from a village five miles from Polomyja. She had been sent with a parcel of grocery to a cottage at no very great distance, but lying apart from the main cluster of hovels, and surrounded by trees.

The day closed in, and her master waited her return anxiously, but as several hours elapsed without any sign of her, he—assisted by the neighbours—went in search of her.

A slight powdering of snow covered the ground, and her footsteps could be traced at intervals where she had diverged from the beaten track. In that part of the road where the trees were thickest, there were marks of two pair of feet leaving the path; but owing to the density of the trees at that spot and to the slightness of the fall of snow, which did not reach the soil, where shaded by the pines, the footprints were immediately lost. By the following morning a heavy fall had obliterated any further traces which day-light might have discovered.

The servant-girl also was never seen again.

During the winter of 1849 the wolves were supposed to have been particularly ravenous, for thus alone did people account for the mysterious disappearances of children.

A little boy had been sent to a fountain to fetch water; the pitcher was found standing by the well, but *the boy had vanished*. The villagers turned out, and those wolves which could be found were despatched.

We have already introduced our readers to Polomyja, although the occurrences above related did not take place among those eight hovels, but in neighbouring villages. The reason for our having given a more detailed account of this cluster of houses—rude cabins they were—will now become apparent.

In May, 1849, the innkeeper of Polomyja missed a couple of ducks, and his suspicions fell upon the beggar who lived there, and whom he held in no esteem, as he himself was a hard-working industrious man, whilst Swiatek maintained himself, his wife, and children by mendicity, although possessed of sufficient arable land to yield an excellent crop of maize, and produce vegetables, if tilled with ordinary care.

As the publican approached the cottage a fragrant whiff of roast greeted his nostrils.

" I'll catch the fellow in the act," said the innkeeper to himself, stealing up to the door, and taking good care not to be observed.

As he threw open the door, he saw the mendicant hurriedly shuffle something under his feet, and conceal it beneath his long clothes. The publican was on him in an instant, had him by the throat, charged him with theft, and dragged him from his seat. Judge of his sickening horror when from beneath the pauper's clothes rolled forth the head of a girl about the age of fourteen or fifteen years, carefully separated from the trunk.

In a short while the neighbours came up. The venerable Swiatek was locked up, along with his wife, his daughter—a girl of sixteen—and a son, aged five.

The hut was thoroughly examined, and the mutilated remains of the poor girl discovered. In a vat were found the legs and thighs, partly raw, partly stewed or roasted. In a chest were the heart, liver, and entrails, all prepared and cleaned, as neatly as though done by a skilful butcher; and, finally, under the oven was a bowl full of fresh blood. On his way to the magistrate of the district, the wretched man flung himself repeatedly on the ground, struggled with his guards, and endeavoured to suffocate himself by gulping down clods of earth and stones, but was prevented by his conductors.

When taken before the Protokoll at Dabkow, he stated that he had already killed and—assisted by his family—eaten six persons : his children, however, asserted most positively that the number was much greater than he had represented, and their testimony is borne out by the fact, that the remains of *fourteen* different caps and suits of clothes, male as well as female, were found in his house.

The origin of this horrible and depraved taste was as follows, according to Swiatek's own confession :—

In 1846, three years previous, a Jewish tavern in the neighbourhood had been burned down, and the host had himself perished in the flames. Swiatek, whilst examining the ruins, had found the half-roasted corpse of the publican among the charred rafters of the house. At that time the old man was craving with hunger, having been destitute of food for some time. The scent and the sight of the roasted flesh inspired him with an uncontrollable desire to taste of it. He tore off a por-

tion of the carcase and satiated his hunger upon it, and
at the same time he conceived such a liking for it, that
he could feel no rest till he had tasted again. His
second victim was the orphan above alluded to; since
then—that is, during the period of no less than three
years—he had frequently subsisted in the same manner,
and had actually grown sleek and fat upon his frightful
meals.

The excitement roused by the discovery of these
atrocities was intense; several poor mothers who had
bewailed the loss of their little ones, felt their wounds
reopened agonisingly. Popular indignation rose to the
highest pitch: there was some fear lest the criminal
should be torn in pieces himself by the enraged people,
as soon as he was brought to trial: but he saved the
necessity of precautions being taken to ensure his safety,
for, on the first night of his confinement, he hanged
himself from the bars of the prison-window.

CHAPTER XV.

ANOMALOUS CASE.—THE HUMAN HYÆNA.

Ghouls—Story from Fornari — Quotation from Apuleius — Incident
mentioned by Marcassus—Cemeteries of Paris violated—Discovery
of Violator—Confession of M. Bertrand.

IT is well known that Oriental romance is full of stories
of violators of graves. Eastern superstition attributes
to certain individuals a passion for unearthing corpses
and mangling them. Of a moonlight night weird forms
are seen stealing among the tombs, and burrowing
into them with their long nails, desiring to reach the
bodies of the dead ere the first streak of dawn compels
them to retire. These ghouls, as they are called, are
supposed generally to require the flesh of the dead for
incantations or magical compositions, but very often
they are actuated by the sole desire of rending the
sleeping corpse, and disturbing its repose. There is

every probability that these ghouls were no mere creations of the imagination, but were actual resurrectionists. Human fat and the hair of a corpse which has grown in the grave, form ingredients in many a necromantic receipt, and the witches who compounded these diabolical mixtures, would unearth corpses in order to obtain the requisite ingredients. It was the same in the middle ages, and to such an extent did the fear of ghouls extend, that it was common in Brittany for churchyards to be provided with lamps, kept burning during the night, that witches might be deterred from venturing under cover of darkness to open the graves.

Fornari gives the following story of a ghoul in his *History of Sorcerers :—*

In the beginning of the 15th century, there lived at Bagdad an aged merchant who had grown wealthy in his business, and who had an only son to whom he was tenderly attached. He resolved to marry him to the daughter of another merchant, a girl of considerable fortune, but without any personal attractions. Abul-Hassan, the merchant's son, on being shown the portrait of the lady, requested his father to delay the marriage till he could reconcile his mind to it. Instead, however, of doing this, he fell in love with another girl, the daughter of a sage, and he gave his father no peace till he consented to the marriage with the object of his affections. The old man stood out as long as he could, but finding that his son was bent on acquiring the hand of the fair Nadilla, and was equally resolute not to accept the rich and ugly lady, he did what most fathers, under such circumstances, are constrained to do, he acquiesced.

The wedding took place with great pomp and ceremony, and a happy honeymoon ensued, which might have been happier but for one little circumstance which led to very serious consequences.

Abul-Hassan noticed that his bride quitted the nuptial couch as soon as she thought her husband was asleep, and did not return to it, till an hour before dawn.

Filled with curiosity, Hassan one night feigned sleep, and saw his wife rise and leave the room as usual. He followed cautiously, and saw her enter a cemetery. By the straggling moonbeams he beheld her go into a tomb ; he stepped in after her.

The scene within was horrible. A party of ghouls were assembled with the spoils of the graves they had violated, and were feasting on the flesh of the long-buried corpses. His own wife, who, by the way, never touched supper at home, played no inconsiderable part in the hideous banquet.

As soon as he could safely escape, Abul-Hassan stole back to his bed.

He said nothing to his bride till next evening when supper was laid, and she declined to eat; then he insisted on her partaking, and when she positively refused, he exclaimed wrathfully,—" Yes, you keep your appetite for your feast with the ghouls!" Nadilla was silent; she turned pale and trembled, and without a word sought her bed. At midnight she rose, fell on her husband with her nails and teeth, tore his throat, and having opened a vein, attempted to suck his blood; but Abul-Hassan springing to his feet threw her down, and with a blow killed her. She was buried next day.

Three days after, at midnight, she re-appeared, attacked her husband again, and again attempted to suck his blood. He fled from her, and on the morrow opened her tomb, burned her to ashes, and cast them into the Tigris.

This story connects the ghoul with the vampire. As will be seen by a former chapter, the were-wolf and the vampire are closely related.

That the ancients held the same belief that the

witches violate corpses, is evident from the third episode in the *Golden Ass* of Apuleius. I will only quote the words of the crier :—

"I pray thee, tell me," replied I, "of what kind are the duties attached to this funeral guardianship?" "Duties!" quoth the crier; "why, keep wide awake all night, with thine eyes fixed steadily upon the corpse, neither winking nor blinking, nor looking to the right nor looking to the left, either to one side or the other, be it even little; for the witches, infamous wretches that they are! can slip out of their skins in an instant and change themselves into the form of any animal they have a mind; and then they crawl along so slyly, that the eyes of justice, nay, the eyes of the sun himself, are not keen enough to perceive them. At all events, their wicked devices are infinite in number and variety; and whether it be in the shape of a bird, or a dog, or a mouse, or even of a common house-fly, that they exercise their dire incantations, if thou art not vigilant in the extreme, they will deceive thee one way or other, and overwhelm thee with sleep; nevertheless, as regards the reward, 'twill be from four to six aurei; nor, although 'tis a perilous service, wilt thou receive more. Nay, hold! I had almost forgotten to give thee a necessary caution. Clearly understand, that if the corpse be not restored to the relatives entire, the deficient pieces of flesh torn off by the teeth of the witches must be replaced from the face of the sleepy guardian."

Here we have the rending of corpses connected with change of form.

Marcassus relates that after a long war in Syria, during the night, troops of lamias, female evil spirits, appeared upon the field of battle, unearthing the hastily buried bodies of the soldiers, and devouring the flesh off their bones. They were pursued and fired upon, and some young men succeeded in killing a considerable number; but during the day they had all of them the forms of wolves or hyænas. That there is a foundation of truth in these horrible stories, and that it is quite possible for a human being to be possessed of a depraved appetite for rending corpses, is proved by an extraordinary case brought before a court-martial in Paris, so late as July 10th, 1849.

The details are given with fulness in the *Annales Medico-psychologiques* for that month and year. They are too revolting for reproduction. I will, however, give an outline of this remarkable case.

In the autumn of 1848, several of the cemeteries in the neighbourhood of Paris were found to have been entered during the night, and graves to have been rifled. The deeds were not those of medical students, for the bodies had not been carried off, but were found lying about the tombs in fragments. It was at first supposed that the perpetration of these outrages must have been a wild beast, but footprints in the soft earth left no doubt that it was a man. Close watch was kept at Père la Chaise; but after a few corpses had been mangled there, the outrages ceased.

In the winter, another cemetery was ravaged, and it was not till March in 1849, that a spring gun which had been set in the cemetery of S. Parnasse, went off during the night, and warned the guardians of the place that the mysterious visitor had fallen into their trap. They rushed to the spot, only to see a dark figure in a military mantle leap the wall, and disappear in the gloom. Marks of blood, however, gave evidence that he had been hit by the gun when it had discharged. At the same time, a fragment of blue cloth, torn from the mantle, was obtained, and afforded a clue towards the identification of the ravisher of the tombs.

On the following day, the police went from barrack

to barrack, inquiring whether officer or man were suffering from a gun-shot wound. By this means they discovered the person. He was a junior officer in the
1st Infantry regiment, of the name of Bertrand.

He was taken to the hospital to be cured of his
wound, and on his recovery, he was tried by court-
martial.

His history was this.

He had been educated in the theological seminary of
Langres, till, at the age of twenty, he entered the army.
He was a young man of retiring habits, frank and cheerful to his comrades, so as to be greatly beloved by them,
of feminine delicacy and refinement, and subject to fits
of depression and melancholy. In February, 1847, as
he was walking with a friend in the country, he came to
a churchyard, the gate of which stood open. The day
before a woman had been buried, but the sexton had not
completed filling in the grave, and he had been engaged
upon it on the present occasion, when a storm of rain
had driven him to shelter. Bertrand noticed the spade
and pick lying beside the grave, and—to use his own
words :—" A cette vue des idées noires me vinrent, j'eus
comme un violent mal de tête, mon cœur battait avec
force, je ne me possédais plus." He managed by some

excuse to get rid of his companion, and then returning to the churchyard, he caught up a spade and began to dig into the grave. " Soon I dragged the corpse out of the earth, and I began to hash it with the spade, without well knowing what I was about. A labourer saw me, and I laid myself flat on the ground till he was out of sight, and then I cast the body back into the grave. I then went away, bathed in a cold sweat, to a little grove, where I reposed for several hours, notwithstanding the cold rain which fell, in a condition of complete exhaustion. When I rose, my limbs were as if broken, and my head weak. The same prostration and sensation followed each attack.

Two days after, I returned to the cemetery, and opened the grave with my hands. My hands bled, but I did not feel the pain; I tore the corpse to shreds, and flung it back into the pit."

He had no further attack for four months, till his regiment came to Paris. As he was one day walking in the gloomy, shadowy, alleys of Père la Chaise, the same feeling came over him like a flood. In the night he climbed the wall, and dug up a little girl of seven years old. He tore her in half. A few days later, he opened the grave of a woman who had died in childbirth, and had lain in the grave for thirteen days. On the 16th November, he dug up an old woman of fifty, and, ripping her to pieces, rolled among the fragments. He did the same to another corpse on the 12th December. These are only a few of the numerous cases of violation of tombs to which he owned. It was on the night of the 15th March that the spring-gun shot him.

Bertrand declared at his trial, that whilst he was in the hospital he had not felt any desire to renew his attempts, and that he considered himself cured of his horrible propensities, for he had seen men dying in the beds around him, and now: "*Je suis guéri, car aujourd'hui j'ai peur d'un mort.*"

The fits of exhaustion which followed his accesses are very remarkable, as they precisely resemble those which followed the berserkir rages of the Northmen, and the expeditions of the Lycanthropists.

The case of M. Bertrand is indubitably most singular and anomalous; it scarcely bears the character of insanity, but seems to point rather to a species of diabolical possession. At first the accesses chiefly followed upon his drinking wine, but after a while they came upon him without exciting cause. The manner in which he mutilated the dead was different. Some he chopped with the spade, others he tore and ripped with his teeth and nails. Sometimes he tore the mouth open and rent the face back to the ears, he opened the stomachs, and pulled off the limbs. Although he dug up the bodies of several men he felt no inclination to mutilate them, whereas he delighted in rending female corpses.

He was sentenced to a year's imprisonment.

CHAPTER XVI.

A SERMON ON WERE-WOLVES.

The discourses of Dr. Johann Geiler—The Sermon—Remarks.

THE following curious specimen of a late mediæval sermon is taken from the old German edition of the discourses of Dr. Johann Geiler von Keysersperg, a famous preacher in Strasbourg. The volume is entitled : —" *Die Emeis.* Dis ist das Büch von der Omeissen, und durch Herr der Künnig ich diente gern. Und sagt von Eigenschafft der Omeissen, und gibt underweisung von der Unholden oder Hexen, und von Gespenst, der Geist, und von dem Wütenden Heer Wunderbarlich."

This strange series of sermons was preached at Strasbourg in the year 1508, and was taken down and written out by a barefooted friar, Johann Pauli, and by him published in 1517. The doctor died on Mid-Lent Sunday, 1510. There is a Latin edition of his sermons, but whether of the same series or not I cannot tell, as I have been unable to obtain a sight of the volume. The German edition is illustrated with bold and clever woodcuts. Among other, there are representations of the Witches' Sabbath, the Wild Huntsman, and a Were-wolf attacking a Man.

The sermon was preached on the third Sunday in Lent. No text is given, but there is a general reference to the gospel for the day. This is the discourse:—*

"What shall we say about were-wolves? for there are were-wolves which run about the villages devouring men and children. As men say about them, they run about full gallop, injuring men, and are called ber-wölff, or wer-wölff. Do you ask me if I know aught about them? I answer, Yes. They are apparently wolves which eat men and children, and that happens on seven accounts:—

1. Esuriem		Hunger.
2. Rabiem		Savageness.
3. Senectutem		Old age.
4. Experientiam		Experience.
5. Insaniem		Madness.
6. Diabolum		The Devil.
7. Deum		God.

"The first happens through hunger; when the wolves

---

* Headed thus:—"Am dritte sontag à faste, occuli, predigt dé doctor vō dē Werwölffenn."

find nothing to eat in the woods, they must come to people and eat men when hunger drives them to it. You see well, when it is very cold, that the stags come in search of food up to the villages, and the birds actually into the dining-room in search of victuals.

" Under the second head, wolves eat children through their innate savageness, because they are savage, and that is (propter locum coitum ferum). Their savageness arises first from their condition. Wolves which live in cold places are smaller on that account, and more savage than other wolves. Secondly, their savageness depends on the season; they are more savage about Candlemas than at any other time of the year, and men must be more on their guard against them then than at other times. It is a proverb, ' He who seeks a wolf at Candlemas, a peasant on Shrove Tuesday, and a parson in Lent, is a man of pluck.' . . . Thirdly, their savageness depends on their having young. When the wolves have young, they are more savage than when they have not. You see it so in all beasts. A wild duck, when it has young poults, you see what an uproar it makes. A cat fights for its young kittens; the wolves do ditto.

" Under the third head, the wolves do injury on

account of their age. When a wolf is old, it is weak and feeble in its legs, so it can't run fast enough to catch stags, and therefore it rends a man, whom it can catch easier than a wild animal. It also tears children and men easier than wild animals, because of its teeth, for its teeth break off when it is very old; you see it well in old women : how the last teeth wobble, and they have scarcely a tooth left in their heads, and they open their mouths for men to feed them with mash and stewed substances.

" Under the fourth head, the injury the were-wolves do arises from experience. It is said that human flesh is far sweeter than other flesh; so when a wolf has once tasted human flesh, he desires to taste it again. So he acts like old topers, who, when they know the best wine, will not be put off with inferior quality.

" Under the fifth head, the injury arises from ignorance. A dog when it is mad is also inconsiderate, and it bites any man; it does not recognize its own lord : and what is a wolf but a wild dog which is mad and inconsiderate, so that it regards no man.

" Under the sixth head, the injury comes of the Devil, who transforms himself, and takes on him the form of a wolf So writes Vincentius in his *Speculum Historiale*.

And he has taken it from Valerius Maximus in the Punic war. When the Romans fought against the men of Africa, when the captain lay asleep, there came a wolf and drew his sword, and carried it off. That was the Devil in a, wolf's form. The like writes William of Paris,— that a wolf will kill and devour children, and do the greatest mischief. There was a man who had the phantasy that he himself was a wolf. And afterwards he was found lying in the wood, and he was dead out of sheer hunger.

"Under the seventh head, the injury comes of God's ordinance. For God will sometimes punish certain lands and villages with wolves. So we read of Elisha, —that when Elisha wanted to go up a mountain out of Jericho, some naughty boys made a mock of him and said, ' O bald head, step up! O glossy pate, step up ! ' What happened ? He cursed them. Then came two bears out of the desert and tore about forty-two of the children. That was God's ordinance. The like we read of a prophet who would set at naught the commands he had received of God, for he was persuaded to eat bread at the house of another. As he went home he rode upon his ass. Then came a lion which slew him and left the ass alone. That was God's ordinance.

Therefore must man turn to God when He brings wild beasts to do him a mischief: which same brutes may He not bring now or evermore.   Amen."

It will be seen from this extraordinary sermon that Dr. Johann Geiler von Keysersperg did not regard were-wolves in any other light than natural wolves filled with a lust for human flesh; and he puts aside altogether the view that they are men in a state of metamorphosis. However, he alludes to this superstition in his sermon on wild-men of the woods, but translates his lycan-thropists to Spain.

THE END.